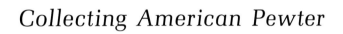

Collecting American Pewter

Teapot of cast brittania. Ten inches tall. Bottom diameter 5⅞ inches. Made by George Richardson, Cranston, Rhode Island, 1830–45.

Collecting American Pewter

Katherine Ebert

Charles Scribner's Sons · New York

Drawings by Sheridan P. Barnard

This book published simultaneously in the United States of America and in
Canada—Copyright under the Berne Convention

1 3 5 7 9 11 13 15 17 19   C/MD   20 18 16 14 12 10 8 6 4 2

Printed in the United States of America

Library of Congress Catalog Card Number 72-12147

SBN 684-13183-8 (cloth)

ACKNOWLEDGMENTS

Since this book, like most others, leans on those which have preceded it, I am indebted to those authors listed as references for their previous contributions. The photographs generously supplied by The Metropolitan Museum of Art, the Brooklyn Museum, the Henry Francis du Pont Winterthur Museum, and other institutions and individuals are acknowledged throughout the book. Special thanks, however, are due to Mr. Edmund P. Hogan, Historical Research Librarian of the International Silver Company, for his help with photographs and information from the daybook of Ashbil Griswold; Mr. Herbert Gebelein of Gebelein Silversmiths of Boston for his information about and photographs of early reproductions; Mr. Israel E. Liverant and Mr. William O. Blaney for their advice and assistance; and Julie B. Leonard of the American Wing, The Metropolitan Museum of Art, for her special efforts.

The drawings of the marks and forms as well as the charts were executed by Mr. Sheridan P. Barnard. Sketching the marks was an especially difficult task which Mr. Barnard carried through with interest, dedication, and obvious skill. His superior artwork adds much to the appearance and usefulness of the book.

On a personal level, I owe thanks to my husband, John, for his contributions to the sections on construction and cleaning and for the many photographs taken by him. My daughter, Carol, contributed by typing the manuscript.

Contents

Collecting American Pewter

Introduction

Collectors collect for many reasons. Some enjoy the element of the chase, the hunting down of the elusive object. Others seek to possess that which they admire for its aesthetic properties. Still others wish to own a bit of history, a part of the life of the past. Yet another group seeks things as an inflation hedge or an investment by buying objects whose supply is finite, and in fact dwindling, as more are removed from circulation by museums. Each of these reasons, in addition to personal and private ones, has its merits.

All collecting is more fruitful if the collector educates himself in his area of special interest. This book is meant to help the beginner and the moderately advanced collector of American pewter. It is not meant to be encyclopedic. Rather than dwelling on the unique or extremely rare, it highlights the typical and more usual. Pewter as a part of history and the life of the past is discussed in the opening chapter. The table of marks at the end of the book is essential for identifying the maker of an object, which in turn tells when, where, and by whom it was made. Knowledge of construction as discussed in Chapter 2 is basic to an understanding of what one sees when examining a piece. Was it cast or spun on a lathe? Is it of eighteenth- or nineteenth-century manufacture?

Pewterware was a vital part of the households of its time and often followed the contemporary fashions of the silversmiths. Pewter was not always a poor humble country cousin. William Will of Philadelphia made tall Federal-style coffee pots equal in dignity and elegance to those of the silver ones of that city. Many photographs of pewter objects made during various periods of the eighteenth and nineteenth centuries enable recognition of American styles and their dates.

Although most collectors have sought those classic items made in the eighteenth and first decades of the nineteenth centuries, it is time for a fresh look at the second quarter of the nineteenth century. This is the period during which a large proportion of the available collectibles were made. Instead of looking for a perpetuation of the eighteenth century in a retread of its designs, one could look for those objects characteristic of the nineteenth century. Such objects show the beginnings of the new industrial age, designs influenced by the new methods and new machines which have particular relevance for our own time.

1

The Rise and Fall of Pewter

Before mass production methods and power-driven machinery brought a vast proliferation of man-made objects, great importance was attached to simple household possessions. In its heyday, pewter was a valued possession. It was so highly regarded that it was specifically bequeathed by will, and often engraved with owners' initials, coats of arms, or commemorative legends and dates. Pewterware came upon the scene high on the social scale in castles and great houses, the new, chic, elegant thing. It replaced woodenware and in its turn was superseded by the newer, more elegant chinaware. With the introduction and then mass production of chinaware, pewter began its descent down the social ladder to end up in remote rural areas until even there it fell into disuse, abandoned in closets, attics, and barns.

European Background

The origin of pewter, a nonstandardized alloy whose main constituent is tin, probably dates back to the Bronze Age. Familiarity with the methods of mining and working tin are necessary to produce bronze, an alloy of copper with tin. The Romans used large quantities of tin to manufacture bronze, and when ready supplies ran out around the Near East, they imported it from Spain, Brittany, and Cornwall. Examples of pewter have been found in various parts of the Roman Empire and over two hundred pieces have been excavated in Britain. Over one-half of these are plates with the remainder consisting of bowls, ewers, cups, and miscellaneous articles all dating from the second to the fourth centuries A.D.

No pewter in Britain can be positively identified as having been made between the fourth and the end of the fourteenth centuries, but it is a matter of record that ecclesiastical vessels and candlesticks were used from the eleventh century on. In 1076 the Council of Winchester forbade the continued use of wooden chalices by the churches in poor parishes and granted instead permission for the consecration of pewter ones. This decision was reversed in 1175 in favor of silver and gold. But in 1194 the churches contributed their silver and gold plate to ransom Richard the Lion-Hearted, so that the pewter communion vessels came back into use. Pewter chalices and patens have been recovered from the graves of ecclesiastics buried in the twelfth and thirteenth centuries. In 1603 the canons ordered that the sacramental wine "should be brought to the table in a sweet standing pot or stoup of pewter, if not of purer metal." Flagons were made to serve this purpose and many are in existence from this time on. On the Continent, many churches used pewter for candlesticks, incense boats, holy-water stoups, chalices, and alms dishes. Jewish ritual accessories such as Hanukkah lamps were also made of pewter, mostly for use in the home.

The fact that pewter was a well-established craft in England by 1348 is indicated by the ordinances of the Craft of Pewterers which regulated quality and workmanship. In 1473, Edward IV granted a royal charter to the Pewterers' Company, which gave the London-based group the power to control activities of pewterers elsewhere in the country. On the Continent pewter vessels and dishes of all types were in widespread use. Germany had a pewter industry at Augsburg in the fourteenth century and Sweden established guild rules in the fifteenth century. Paintings by Jan Steen, Franz Hals, Jan Vermeer, and Jan van Eyck often show pewter flagons, dishes, basins, and tankards.

Hard drinking was customary in Europe in medieval times so that measures, flagons, tankards, and mugs (pots) were in great demand. Flagons, a class of large vessels from which a liquid is poured into smaller and more convenient sizes for individual use, were first made of wood and leather. As pewter was introduced it was used side by side with the older containers, which were gradually replaced. In turn, the pewter mugs and tankards gradually gave way to silver in the homes of the wealthy, although a pewter tankard was still a prized possession in the homes of the less affluent well into the eighteenth century. In the sixteenth century the House of Commons made it mandatory for wine and spirits to be accurately measured. The units were specified in a succession of laws and vast numbers of pewter measures were made to these various standards in an extensive array of sizes.

In medieval times, woodenware, in the form of platters, trenchers, cups, and bowls was the common household tableware. Pewter was added to this in the homes of the rich after the Restoration. Samuel Pepys, in his diary entry for October 29, 1663, complained, understandably, that at a banquet at London's Guild Hall "it was unpleasing that we had no napkins nor change of trenchers and drunk out of earthen pitchers and wooden dishes." As England became wealthier, the average man was able to afford more possessions and pewter came into general use in the households of those of moderate means by the early part of the eighteenth century. Pewter plates were often proudly displayed in open cupboards or kept for use only on special occasions. This helps explain the unexpected fact that occasionally an old pewter plate appears in almost unused condition.

The amount of pewter used in great houses can be established by the examination of early household inventories. One made on September 30, 1624, at Speke Hall, Lancashire, lists the pewter in "The Store House" which includes eight and a half dozen plates and dishes of various sizes, basins, ewers, and other miscellaneous dishes whose total weight is "34 score pounds, and 3 odd pounds," almost a third of a ton of metal. The inventory continues to list more in the storehouse, the kitchen, the buttery, and a small amount "for the servants." The enormous quantity and variety with "great flagons," "cannes of London pewter," candlesticks, "chamber pottes," saltcellars, and porringers show its important role in the daily life of this mansion. Although no individual makers are mentioned, it is significant that the London origin of the cans or mugs is specified. This underscores the prestige of the London makers.

The inventory made in 1612 of Dean Castle in Ayrshire lists seventy pewter plates and one dozen pewter trenchers. As so often happens when a new material is introduced, it enters in the shape and form of the object it is intended to replace. Thus the earliest pewter plates were made in the form of the square wooden trenchers in common use at the time. These and other inventories of great English houses enumerate relatively few drinking vessels. It is likely that glass displaced pewter for this purpose in wealthy households in the late sixteenth century.

Pewter in America

At the time of the settlement of Plymouth Colony in America the customary tableware was of wood with pewter regarded as a luxury. In the Massachusetts Bay colony a detailed inventory was required in order to settle the estate of a deceased person. These records supply accurate descriptions of the contents of the houses of this period. The use of pewter in America by 1633 is firmly established by the inventory of Will Wright of Plymouth Colony which lists seven pewter platters ("3 great ones and 4 little ones"), three porringers, "2 pint potts" (mugs), one pewter flagon, and two pewter cups. The widow Sarah Dillingham died at Ipswich in 1635 with forty and a half pounds of pewter as part of her substantial estate. Since the metal itself was of value, the weight was often included in the listing.

An examination of the inventories of rural Suffolk County, Massachusetts, of which Boston was the county seat, at approximately twenty-five-year intervals until 1775 shows the steady progression from treen to pewter and eventually to chinaware. These rural inhabitants were not so quick to adopt the latest fashion as were the cosmopolitan residents of Boston. Many utensils of iron, brass, and earthenware are included in these early inventories as well as pewter in the form of platters, serving dishes, basins (for serving food), salts, baby bottles, mugs, porringers, and chamber pots. Pewter dining plates were not in general use until well after 1700. John Ffarington of Dedham in 1676 left

> 9 pewter dishes & a bason
> Three pewter: ptts: two cups a vinegar
> a Suckling bottle and some old porringers . . .
> Trenchers . . . spoons
> nine small wood dishes . . . three bowls & foure trayes . . .
> Earthen vessels . . . two wooden bottles

These "pewter dishes" are most likely serving dishes rather than dinner plates, since dishes and plates are listed as separate items in most cases.

Pewter baby bottle or suckling bottle. Thomas Danforth Boardman, c. 1805. (The Metropolitan Museum of Art. Gift of Joseph France, 1943)

6

Toward the turn of the century pewter plates begin to appear, although wooden trenchers are still listed. This trend continues through the first quarter of the eighteenth century as the use of pewter plates becomes more widespread. The inventory of David Cushing of Hingham taken in 1724 no longer lists any trenchers but does enumerate one dozen pewter plates. John Randall of Weymouth in 1730 left five pewter platters, eight plates, three large basins, one quart pot, one pint pot, one porringer, and one suckling bottle. However, wooden plates were not yet altogether discarded, for the inventories of the estates of Ebenezer Jones of Dorchester in 1735 and Jacob Williams of Roxbury in 1737 both contain them.

Toward the middle of the eighteenth century china plates start to displace pewter among the wealthy, while pewter displaces woodenware among the middle class. As the shift from wood to pewter was first made by the wealthy, so the shift from pewter to chinaware was first made by them also. In 1749, Ebenezer Dudley of Roxbury had a house and land valued at 7,580 pounds sterling. His household furnishings were predictably in keeping with this substantial estate, containing no pewter but instead a large variety of china:

> 10 China plates, 2 small punch Bowls, 2 milk Bowls,
> 16 Cups 2 Breakfast Bowls & Creampotts
> 6 Bowls and Saucers and Bowl & Tea Pott
> 12 China plates & 2 pickle Plates

At the same time, Daniel Weld of Roxbury had a house and land valued at 767 pounds sterling, about one-tenth that of Mr. Dudley. Mr. Weld's estate contained a considerable amount of pewter including one and a half dozen plates, twenty-one wooden plates, but no china at all.

By 1774, some twenty-five years later, pewter is found mainly in the kitchen while china appears in the dining room in those houses large enough to have one. Aaron Davis, Jr., of Roxbury, merchant, in 1774 had "glass and china in the closset" and in the kitchen "74 pounds of Pewter." The china is for display and special occasions, much as the pewter was earlier.

The earliest record of an American pewterer is Richard Graves, who settled in Salem, Massachusetts, in 1635. Fewer than twenty Americans were engaged in the craft prior to 1750. The slow start was due to English trade restrictions and competition. The chart shows the vast quantities of pewterware imported into this country from England and partially explains why so much of the pewter found here is of English origin. In the five-year period from the beginning of 1760 to the beginning of 1765 pewterware worth over 125,000 pounds sterling was shipped here from English ports—more than two and a half times the value of the furniture shipped during the same period. The increase reflects the increase in population, of course, but from the 1700–05 to the 1760–65

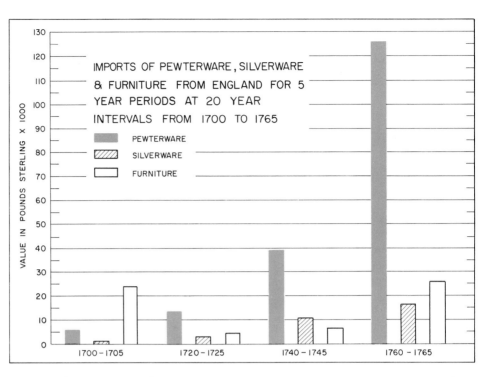

Imports of pewterware, silverware, and furniture from England for 5-year periods at 20-year intervals from 1700 to 1765.

period the value of the English furniture imported only doubled while that of pewterware increased tenfold. An advertisement for these products in the Boston *Evening Post* of July 26, 1756, shows the tremendous variety offered: "London pewter dishes, plates, basons, porringers, breakfast bowls, tablespoons, pint and quart pots, cans, tankards, butter cups, newest fashion teapots, table salts, suckling bottles, plates and dishes covers, cullenders, soap kettles, new fashion roased [*sic*] plates, communion beakers and flagons and measures."

The scarcity of existing American pewter compared with English is noted by Mr. Kerfoot who in his pioneering book on American pewter written in 1924 estimated that he came across one hundred and twenty-five English plates for each American one. Mr. Laughlin in his definitive and scholarly work estimates the frequency slightly greater than one in a hundred. Thus the much higher price for American pewter today compared with English is not just a function of chauvinism but a reflection of its scarcity.

By the time of the Revolution, pewter's upper-class status for dining was usurped by china. A great impetus was given to the use of china by the fad for tea-drinking which swept through England and America. Following the establishment of the Dutch East India Company in 1609 and the British East India Company in 1631, a flood of Oriental wares appeared in European markets and with it the introduction of tea. Samuel Pepys in his diary entry of September 25, 1660, records, "I did send for a cup of tea, a china drink, of which I had never drunk before." Mugs or tankards of pewter or silver were satisfactory for the drinking of ale or cider, but hardly appropriate for the delicate, exotic flavor of tea. Fashion prescribed dainty porcelain cups, the first of which were without handles. A whole ritual with the accompanying equipage of tea tables, teapots, sugar bowls, and creamers was developed.

China was imported into this country before 1775, but it was not until after the Revolution that the deluge came and signaled the end of the first period of pewter-making in this country. Our merchants became free at last to trade with countries other than England and were quick to exploit the possibilities of the Far East. The great era of the American-China trade was under way. The *Empress of China* left New York for Canton on February 22, 1784, and by 1790 twenty-eight American ships had followed. Elias Hasket Derby of Salem alone had sent out forty-nine ventures before 1800. The American-China trade became the most profitable branch of American shipping which culminated in the development of the clipper ships in the 1840's. While it flourished, tons of porcelain, tea, spices, and exotic luxuries entered the ports along the eastern seaboard.

As if the booming China trade were not enough of a problem to the pewterer, the English Staffordshire pottery factories were improving their products to compete with the Oriental wares and these were imported in large quantities by vessels engaged in the cotton trade. New England ships carried lumber, potatoes, hay, and furniture to the southern cotton ports, usually Charleston, Savannah, Mobile, or New Orleans. There the cargo was sold and cotton taken aboard bound for Liverpool. In Liverpool the cotton was sold and a miscellaneous cargo of English goods was selected to yield the best profit at the moment. Pottery was a prominent component of such cargo.

By 1775 Josiah Wedgwood's pottery became a highly skilled industrial activity utilizing power-driven machinery. It was this mechanization which brought about the production of vast quantities of china at popular prices that finally drove pewter out of the homes of the middle class as the daily household dinnerware.

The pewtering craft in the eighteenth century was essentially medieval in its methods. The designer and craftsman was one and the same and learning was by the long-drawn-out process of apprenticeship. When the market for dinnerware started to erode about 1790, the industry in England, and later in America, responded with the gradual introduction of brittania, a harder variation of pewter invented in England. A new phase was begun with the development of mechanized fabrication methods which could be used readily with the new hard metal. Furthermore, it took a fine high polish and was ideal for the teapots and coffee pots which were in great demand. This aspect of pewter has sometimes caused it to be termed "poor man's silver."

Large quantities of brittaniaware were made in the first half of the nineteenth century in such forms as teapots, coffeepots, sugar bowls, creamers, candlesticks, cruet stands, water pitchers, porringers, whale oil lamps, chalices, and flagons. As the demand grew the makers changed from one-or two-man shops to large factories such as the Reed and Barton plant in Taunton, Massachusetts. At first the lathes were small hand-powered types, but the machinery scale grew and developed into full-fledged factories using steam and water power. When the designs were developed by the owner or his helper they had a simple American flavor, but as the Victorian era advanced, designs became fancier as the factories rushed to copy the latest English styles.

The final blow was the invention and patenting of electroplating of silver in the 1840's. After the Civil War unplated pewter or brittania was a thing of the past. Pewter's ignominious state is shown by the description of a child's tea service in the 1875 Christmas catalogue of James W. Tufts of Boston:

> . . . These are made of the best quality of Brittania Metal. . . . They are all heavily silver plated, and the milk pitcher, sugar and slop bowls, cups and saucers are lined with gold.

"Dregs in the Cup or Fortune Telling," painting by William S. Mount, 1838, showing brittania teapot. (Courtesy of the New-York Historical Society)

2

Metal, Construction, and Marks

Isolated from the sources of raw materials, the colonial pewterer in America was at a disadvantage compared with his English counterpart. The pre-Revolutionary English government sought to protect the large export business of finished pewterware to America by imposing taxes on tin, the principal constituent of pewter, and by forbidding the colonists to trade directly with the tin-producing countries of the Orient. The most readily available source of the needed metal was from used pewter articles that were scrapped. The high cost of the molds plus the uncertain supply of raw materials dampened the growth of the industry and many who went into the trade did so only on a part-time basis.

The Metal

After the Revolution, however, this changed and Americans were free to trade with anyone on their own terms. Account books of the early nineteenth century mention four or five sources of tin:

> English tin—from Cornwall but also some from Devonshire and Wales
> Banca tin—from Bangka, now part of Indonesia
> "Streights" tin—from Malacca near the tip of the Malay Peninsula bordering the Malacca Strait
> Spanish tin—from the Galician Mountains separating Spain and Portugal
> India tin—probably from various parts of the Orient

Among other constituents of pewter were bismuth which was obtained from deposits in England, copper and antimony from the Orient and Europe, and lead which came from Europe. Individual pewterers had preferences as to the source of their tin, probably due to the fact that impurities gave each somewhat different physical properties. Through-

One of a group of receipts from the shop of Lemma Bartholomew in Plainfield, Connecticut. William Danforth of Middletown bought old pewter from Bartholomew as stated in this receipt dated August 14, 1804. He bought 1,078¾ pounds of it and, in addition, paid Bartholomew a commission for collecting it. (Private collection)

In this same group of documents are receipts for the purchase of pewterware from Samuel Danforth of Hartford for resale by Bartholomew. In turn, Danforth bought, among other things, old pewter, lead, cheesecloth, and beeswax. All of this was charged and the account was settled with the addition of a small amount of cash on March 15, 1803. (Private collection)

out the pewter and brittania periods used pewter from worn and broken pieces furnished a substantial amount of the pewterer's raw material but the availability of new metals after the Revolution gave the home trade a tremendous boost.

Neither English nor American pewter has fixed proportions for its ingredients. All compositions have tin as the principal component with copper, antimony, and bismuth added to give strength, hardness, and resonance. Bismuth, however, lowered the melting point and made the metal brittle. It was later replaced by antimony, which did not have these disadvantages and in addition produced a ductile alloy that could take a high polish with a silvery luster. Early pewter, up to the last quarter of the eighteenth century, contained lead almost universally; the more lead the lower the cost, but the poorer the quality. Some workers added zinc to the mix. The exact recipe used by a particular pewterer depended on what was available, the end use, and his own preferences due to bias or some advantage in fabrication or sales appeal.

Up until about 1815, most of the American pewter continued to include lead. The formulas for the new English alloys were secrets and not widely known here. Mr. Laughlin had assays made of some typical late eighteenth-century American pewter, which are recorded in his book, *Pewter in America*. The results are given below:

	Tin	Copper	Lead	Antimony
Joseph Danforth plate	88.52%	0.67	8.33	2.47
Edward Danforth plate	88.43%	0.97	8.39	2.15

When china and earthenware began making heavy inroads in the pewterer's domain in England from the 1770's on, the trade there responded by developing new harder, more silvery and lustrous alloys that were also easier to keep bright. Some English makers had long since used similar alloys for their most expensive products. This new class of alloys, or newly popularized alloys, free of lead, was called brittania metal, probably in imitation of the Brittania silver formula, a very high grade of silver used in England from 1697 to 1720. As in the case of pewter, there are no fixed proportions for brittania metal. *The Tinman's Manual and Builder's and Mechanics' Handbook* by R. Butts, published in 1860, lists some formulas used at that time:

	Tin	Copper	Antimony
Good brittania metal	92%	1.85%	6.15%
Brittania metal for casting	93	1.8	5.2
Brittania metal for spinning	93.5	2.8	3.7

Some of the formulas also contained bismuth and zinc. It is remarkable that such small differences in the formula between pewter and brittania should make such a marked difference in the properties of the alloy.

In the 1790's and early 1800's, finished English brittaniaware was imported into America, where it met no native competition since the formula had not yet been developed here. One of the first to do so was Thomas Danforth Boardman of Hartford, Connecticut. In his autobiography he said that he first heard of regulus of antimony in 1805 and was able to acquire a few pounds of it. Regulus of antimony is the more or less impure metal formed beneath the slag in the process of smelting and reducing the ore. In 1806 he had success and reported (corrected):

> I received a lot of English tin from a pewterer in Philadelphia with orders to make it into teapots just as it was. I cast the pots but could not turn them the metal was so soft the chips would (?). I melted them down and added 2 or 3% copper which had been tried before and as much R. antimony—which proved to be the right thing. The pots were the best I had ever made. From what I could learn very few teapots had been made in New England and these were very clumsey. With the proper proportions of regulus of antimony and copper the ware would finish up equal to the English, bright around the solderings of the trimmings so the merchants who had imported the article considered them equal to English. Of course we had orders from manufacturers of pewter ware to furnish them with our teapots from Philadelphia, Providence, Hartford, and to merchants in New York, Philadelphia, New Haven, Albany, Utica, Newburgh, Providence, Newport, and Boston. One house would order 50 dozen at a time. One ordered 3,000 within 6 months.

At about the same time, an obscure and very young pewterer in Beverly, Massachusetts, by the name of Philip Lee was also using what was essentially brittania metal. He did not prosper and in 1812 sold out to Israel Trask, who had decided to forgo his profession of silversmith to make brittania teapots in response to the demand created by the cut-off of English supplies during the War of 1812. By 1820, the secret formula had leaked from the Boardman shop and shortly thereafter was in general use.

Today the style and construction of brittaniaware is often the key in identifying a piece as being made of brittania metal rather than pewter. The passage of time has obscured the silvery sheen which made the metal so popular. Machine buffing restores it but this is, of course, an unthinkable approach to an antique. Since brittania is much stronger than pewter, it is often formed in thin walls using construction techniques such as spinning or seaming rather than casting. However, articles were also formed by casting all through the period. Styles were influenced somewhat by the physical properties of the metal but to a greater extent reflect the taste and fashions of the period in which they were made.

Fabrication of pewter and brittania objects in America can be broken down into two time periods. The first, and earlier, is the manufacture of items by casting in molds. A later technique in the second period formed parts using cast sheets of brittania that were often smoothed and made denser by passage between steel rollers. Early pieces, before 1825, are cast with few exceptions but later products are either cast or fabricated from sheet.

The casting molds used in America were nearly always made of brass or bronze and were very expensive. They were a highly valued and important part of the pewterer's capital equipment and when he died or went out of business they were passed on to others in his family or sold on the open market. An advertisement to sell molds appeared in the April 11, 1737, issue of the *Boston Gazette*:

> A good set of Pewterer's Molds to be Sold either in
> whole or in part, very cheap, by Mr. Oxenbridge Thatcher.

Some molds were brought to America by pewterers who left England or the Continent for a new life. Some were also made in America by American braziers many of whom were also pewterers. A notice in the *Connecticut Courant* for November 23, 1773, clearly establishes this. Samuel Hamlin announces that his partnership with Thomas Danforth II of Middletown is dissolved, that he is moving to Providence and that he

> . . . has nearly completed a set of moulds, of the newest
> and neatest fashions, and flatters himself that they will
> on tryal give universal satisfaction. . . .

Except for simple items such as plates, most pewter articles required several molds. A complicated piece such as a tulip-shaped tankard might require at least seven separate molds:

1. Cover mold
2. Thumbpiece mold
3. Hinge mold
4. Upper body mold
5. Lower body mold
6. Bottom mold
7. Handle mold

Tall altar candlesticks formerly used in a church in eastern Pennsylvania. Example of an object made using molds brought from Europe. Height: 22½ inches. Johann Christopher Heyne, 1756–80. (Courtesy of the Henry Francis du Pont Winterthur Museum)

Basin mold for 10-inch basins. Basins, like plates, required only one mold. Spoon mold for casting spoons with round bowl and trifid handle. Both eighteenth century. (Courtesy of the Brooklyn Museum)

Since each of these molds was very expensive, the pewterer tried to use each one for as many different articles as possible, such as the same lid for two different items, the base of one item as the lid for another, or the tankard mold used as part of the taller flagon. The high cost of new molds limited the range of products a pewterer was able to make, so he rounded out his line by selling English products and by buying from other American pewterers.

Articles made from multiple castings were joined by soldering or fusing. In soldering, the pieces were held together mechanically and molten solder was applied to the joint using a hot soldering iron and rosin flux. The hot solder then bridged the gap between the pieces so that, when the solder fused to the pewter and hardened, the two sections were firmly joined. Instead of a soldering iron, some pewterers used a blowpipe and a candle flame to apply the heat. Later a whale-oil lamp was substituted for the candle, and still later, in the 1850's, a gas flame was used.

The previously mentioned *Tinman's Manual* gives the proportions for a suitable solder as about 60% tin and 40% lead, which is close to the alloy with the lowest melting point. Such an alloy is the easiest to use in managing to melt the solder without melting away the pewter, also largely tin and lead, and also with a low melting point. Unfortunately, such solder is duller than the pewter, so for joining in conspicuous places the meticulous craftsman often used a solder with a higher tin content or pieces of pewter itself. Successful use of high-tin solders required great skill.

Fusing, or joining two pieces by melting the metal of the areas to be joined without the addition of solder, was sometimes used on tankards and other items, but its main use was for joining sections where maxi-

Covered water pitcher and sugar bowl with interchangeable lids. Shows the frugality of the pewterer in using the same lid mold for separate items. Pitcher made by Parks Boyd, working 1795–1819. Sugar bowl unmarked but assumed to be by same maker since it has lid identical to marked pitcher. (Courtesy of the Brooklyn Museum)

mum strength was required. This was the most common way to attach a porringer handle to its bowl, and was called "burning on." First the porringer bowl was formed and finished and then the handle mold was held onto the cold bowl while molten pewter was poured into the other end of the mold. The hot pewter melted part of the bowl and formed a homogeneous joint. A tinker's dam, a stopping rag of linen or burlap filled with wet sand, was pushed against the inside of the bowl during this process to cool and maintain the shape of the bowl. The metal softened sufficiently to leave the imprint of the cloth, the linen mark, on the inside of the porringer bowl. Evidence of this can be seen in the photograph.

Pewter directly from the mold often had voids and a rough surface which had to be finished to make it attractive. The voids in the casting were filled using a soldering iron with pewter as solder. The excess metal was removed from the flat surfaces with a large, flat, coarse-cut file or float. After this initial rough-finishing, the maker's mark was stamped on the piece. Next was the skimming, which was done with a special tool of sharp steel at the end of a wooden holder. The operation was performed by holding the tool against the article as it rotated on a lathe so that small amounts of metal were removed in a spiral pattern. Evidence of this first skimming can be seen on the bottoms of pieces that were not finished further as shown on the porringer base in the photograph.

Interior of porringer showing linen mark left when casting on handle. (Private collection)

17

Bottom of porringer showing spiral marks left by skimming operation. (Private collection)

A final burnishing or buffing operation was then undertaken. Burnishing was done while the piece was still in the lathe by holding a burnishing tool against the object as it was rapidly turned. The tool had a polished stone or steel face that pushed and flattened small roughnesses still left on the surface. This process did not remove metal. Soapy water was sometimes poured over the burnishing tool to lubricate and cool both the work and the tool. After 1825, in the second period, buffing was the final finishing operation, either after the burnishing or the skimming. Buffing was a polishing method that used a rapidly rotating buff which was pressed against the surface to be polished. The buff was a disk made of pieces of hide or cloth and usually used with a finely ground abrasive polishing powder. As a final step, decorative lines were often cut into the rim and well of plates and on the outside of hollow-ware.

Some details of fabrication and finishing have been lost with time and as a result several points are in dispute. One of these is whether the maker's mark was stamped before finishing only to have it damaged in the final operation, or whether it was added as the final touch of proud workmanship. In fact, it was probably done both ways depending on the piece. The great emphasis put on a maker's mark by collectors was certainly not the case at the time of manufacture. The household inventories rarely specify the maker of the pewter but describe it only with respect to condition, as old or new. Infrequent references are to "London Made," which indicates the high regard for the London guild but not usually a particular maker. It seems likely that the American pewterer was aiming primarily for a well-finished piece, even at the expense of damaging his mark somewhat. The large number of unmarked pieces of patently American origin and of fine workmanship would bolster this conclusion.

18

The demarcation date of 1825 between the old cast pewter and the later hard metal is chosen somewhat arbitrarily. It could have been 1815 or even 1835 because the changes in the metal and the fabricating techniques were not abrupt. T. D. Boardman first used the new alloy in 1805 and by the 1820's many others had followed suit. New techniques were slower in spreading as most pewterers were still casting their wares until the mid-1830's.

The last quarter of the eighteenth century had brought basic changes to silversmithing by the introduction of rolled sheet silver. The new brittania was hard enough to use in this way, but, unlike silver, did not work-harden and require fire annealing. Beginning about 1812, Israel Trask, with his background as a silversmith, used cast and rolled sheets of brittania in a process called seaming. The sheet was cut to shape over a cylinder and then soldered at the seam. The photograph shows the seam on the interior of one of his most successful designs, the lighthouse tea or coffeepot. Oliver Trask and Eben Smith, also working in Beverly, Massachusetts, with Israel Trask, used this method but it did not become a standard or widely used method of fabrication brittania. The lighthouse-style pots made by other makers are not generally formed this way and, in fact, are usually cast.

Lighthouse-style teapot made by seaming and having bright-cut decoration. Height: 11 inches. Israel Trask, 1813–35. (Private collection)

19

Interior of Trask pot showing lengthwise seam behind spout.

Detail of bright-cut engraving on same Trask pot.

Illustration in Godey's Lady's Book,
March 1853, showing a drop press.

About 1827 Babbitt and Crossman started using a stamping technique
to form various parts for their line of wares. Stamping, which had been
used in England for many years, consisted of shaping a flat sheet of
metal between a male and a female die. At first, the force was supplied
by a screw press but the faster drop press became more common. The
cut from the March 1853 *Godey's Lady's Book* article on "Everyday
Actualities" shows a contemporary drop press. Often a successive series
of ever deeper dies had to be used for deep-drawn items in order to
keep the metal from wrinkling or breaking. Babbitt and Crossman took
pride in the finish of their products and tried continuously to improve
the rolling equipment used to produce the sheet metal from the cast
bar. They were the first to try a steam engine to drive the steel rollers,
but this was unsatisfactory and they were forced to return to water
power.

Another new manufacturing technique was introduced in America in
1834 when William P. Crossman of the Taunton Britannia Manufacturing
Company was granted a United States patent for a spinning process.
This was "for an improved process for manufacturing Tea Pots, and
other articles of Brittania Ware," and was similar to techniques used
in England after 1820. A cut from the March 1853 issue of *Godey's Lady's
Book* shows a spinner in a gas chandelier factory with a remote source

Illustration in Godey's Lady's Book, March 1853, showing a spinner at work.

of belt-driven power. The accompanying description of forming from the cut blank, a brass disk with a mounting hole in the center, is similar to the technique used for brittania.

> This round plate has a hole cut in its center; it is then taken to the turning-lathe, and the brass plate [brittania in our case] before described is secured by its center to the wooden frame. The "spinner" then smears the surface of the plate with soap, to make his tools work easily. The lathe is set in motion, and the wooden block, with the brass [brittania in our case] plate attached, is made to revolve rapidly; the spinner, then, by means of a smooth iron tool which has a long wooden handle, presses the plate over the wooden mold until it covers closely every part of the pattern. This forms a "bowl" of any shape which may be desired.

Since wooden blocks or patterns were cheap to make and easy to change with the fashions, spinning became popular among manufacturers, being widely used after 1840.

The unwanted portions from the spinning and stamping operations were cut off on a lathe. The various sections were then assembled and soldered together in the same way as the cast sections in the old method. Skimming, honing, and buffing gave the piece the desired finish. The tell-tale rings from the spinning process were left on the interior surfaces of such articles as tea and coffeepots, where they can often be clearly seen. Spouts and handles continued to be cast throughout this period. The design and component sections of the tall teapots by A. Porter and

A. Griswold are very similar, although one is cast and the other spun.

As the business flourished in the 1840's, larger and improved machines were used and the size of the workforce increased, becoming factories as we know them today. Other techniques such as shearing and stamping were developed to form flat shapes for tea services. Pewtering as a craft was dead. Pewterware became a manufactured ware with many factories converting to silverplate in the 1850's.

Tall, elongated, pear-shaped teapot made by spinning. Height: 12½ inches. Allen Porter, 1830-38. (Private collection)

Similar pot made by casting. Height: 12 inches. Ashbil Griswold, 1807-35. (Private collection)

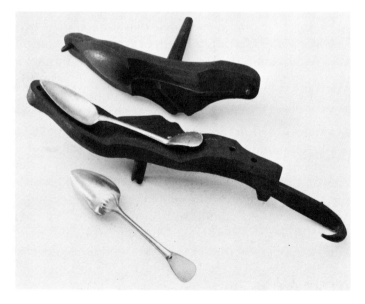

Late spoon mold patented by W. Mix in 1848 for an improved method of making spoons with shanks strengthened by the insertion of steel wires. (Courtesy of the International Silver Company)

23

Marks

There is little that pleases a collector more than learning the when, where, and whom of his latest aquisition. American pewter, unlike many other antiques, is often marked in a way that can place it in time and place of origin. Such associations are inherently more interesting than the anonymity of so many old objects, so that a collector pays much more for a marked piece than for a comparable unmarked piece. The condition and rarity of the mark are important considerations in the price, along with the form and condition of the piece itself.

For the background of American marks one must again turn to England. The London guild which calls itself in all seriousness *The Worshipful Company of Pewterers* originated in 1348 in order to regulate the quality, workmanship, and other aspects of the pewterers' trade. There is a reference to the use of marks in 1474 and in 1503 marking became mandatory. In 1549, a pewter touchplate was started which the active members were required to stamp with their particular marks and which was then kept in the guild hall as a record. The great London fire of 1666 destroyed the old plates, but new ones were again begun. Five are currently in existence recording all the official London makers from 1666 to about 1825 (plus one straggler in 1913). Similar plates exist in Edinburgh, Scotland. All sorts of designs appear on the London plates including animals, birds, and hands. After 1720, many of the marks were framed by pillars which became a popular device in the colonies.

In addition to the primary marks recorded on the touchplates, various types of secondary marks also appear. The crowned rose was used after 1671 by the London Guildhall as a mark of the hall and was stamped on items for export to other parts of England or abroad. Crowned "X" and "X" were used to indicate high-quality metal. Some men included marks which stated that the piece was made in London or of superior metal. Pseudo hallmarks, three or four small shieldlike stamps in a row, were used by some English makers to imply quality through association with similar marks used by silversmiths. The pewter marks do not have the significance of the silver ones and were resented by the silversmiths as pretentious and misleading. Owners' initials were commonly stamped on English articles.

With the enormous amount of English pewter coming into America during the first half of the eighteenth century, all of these marking styles and customs were carefully copied by the American pewterer. London pewter was highly regarded as the standard of excellence for the western world, so this reputation was exploited by the Americans who marked their wares with a London stamp and with London symbols which capitalized on the illiteracy of the times. The rose, crowned rose, lion rampant, and gateway framed by pillars were adopted by American workers, as well as pseudo hallmarks and the label "Made in London."

24

Rose and crown mark with
"London" used by unidenti-
fied American maker or
makers, c. 1740-80.

Lion in gateway with pseudo-
hallmarks touch of Thomas
Danforth II, of Middletown,
Connecticut, 1755-82.

One of the eagle marks of
Samuel Danforth of Hart-
ford, Connecticut, c. 1800.

After the Revolution the rose, crown, and lion rampant were out and
eagles were in. The eagle designs were frequently copied from similar
devices used on the coins issued by the new republic in 1792. Indians
and eagles used on the coinage of some states such as the Massachusetts
cents of 1787 were picked up by some. Most of the eagle marks are
circular and only one, that of Nathaniel Austin, uses side pillars. Pseudo
hallmarks continued to be used until about 1810.

The high water mark of the post-Revolutionary eagle marks was about
1815 and then almost completely disappeared after 1835. The eagles were
replaced by name marks which had been used to some extent in the
eighteenth century but became more widespread in the nineteenth. At
first the names were punched in with a die which punched in the metal

Die-stamped name mark of Allen Porter, 1830–38.   *Incised mark of Reed & Barton, 1840 or later.*

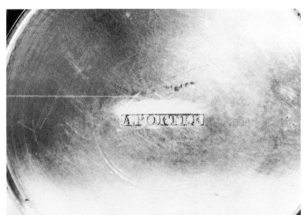

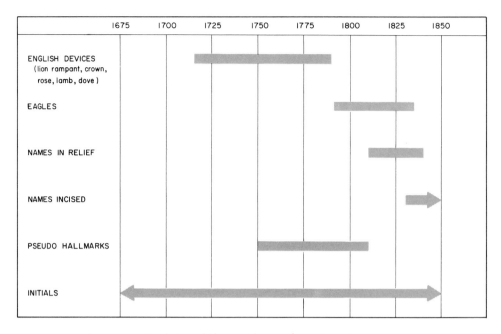

	1675	1700	1725	1750	1775	1800	1825	1850

ENGLISH DEVICES
(lion rampant, crown, rose, lamb, dove)

EAGLES

NAMES IN RELIEF

NAMES INCISED

PSEUDO HALLMARKS

INITIALS

Approximate dates of the marks used on American pewter.

around the letters, leaving them in relief in the fashion of the early makers. Later, after about 1830, the names only were punched so that the letters were incised into the metal. Initials were used throughout the American pewter period from 1650 to 1850 but were not common. Apparently, the pewterer left this form of marking to the silversmiths.

Many American pieces are not marked, probably because there was no guild here which required it in order to enforce standards of quality. Perhaps marking was omitted through haste, oversight, the lack of a stamping die, or because the item was intended for resale by another merchant. It was not unusual to mark only one piece of a matched set. Such unmarked pieces form the basis of assigning makers by attribution through careful comparison with the form and dimensions of a marked piece. It is often stated that all unmarked pieces are American. They could not be English, since English pieces were required to be marked. This is putting naive faith in the power of a regulating agency to regulate behavior. The London Guild was not always effective in country areas and as the use of pewter declined in England, the guild declined as an effective deterrent. The last significant touch on the London plate was struck ca. 1823, which indicates that the guild was long past the prime of influence by then. In fact, large numbers of English pewter pieces occur unmarked.

3

First Period   1700–1825

It is not possible to select a particular date at which the characteristics of pewter making changed in America so that the date of 1825 is only one point in a period of transition. The old period begins with the complete dependence on European tools and equipment, training, designs, and methods. Designs persisted here beyond the time when they became obsolete in Europe, for the American pewterer could not afford to change his molds so readily. The old method of making pewter was essentially that of a medieval craft developed by trial and error, learned by "see" and "do." Science was a philosophy, an intellectual exercise, and not concerned with the improvement of physical things or processes. It was not until scientific methods were applied to the making of things that pewter making became an industry using power other than human or animal.

Early pewter objects were made in a multiplicity of forms for household and ecclesiastical uses. Some of these forms are still unknown to us even though their existence is documented by listings in household or shop inventories. A description of some of the articles of most interest to collectors is given here, although some are now so rare outside of museums that they are available only occasionally and then only at very high prices.

Household Pewter

Plates and Dishes

During the First Period, plates, dishes, and basins constituted the bulk of the pewterer's trade. The examples that exist range from unique to readily available. Although no marked American plates are really cheap, many are within the reach of a collector of moderate means. No collection is complete without some good marked plates and it is among these that specimens of marked pieces by early makers can most readily be obtained.

"Plates" and "dishes" are imprecise terms in modern usage and will be used here without clear distinction between them. In general, plates were for individual service and dishes for holding food from which individual servings were "dished" out. The great preponderance of existing plates are shallow and in the eight-inch diameter range, roughly seven and a half to eight and a half inches. These were the individual dinner plates, although they seem small to us today for this purpose. Other plates and dishes may be smaller than five inches in diameter, or as large as nineteen.

Our earliest pewterers were trained in England and must have brought their molds and tools with them. Thus it is to be expected that our earliest plates look like English ones of the time. One of the earliest of these is a unique broad-brim plate with a deep well and hammered all over, made by Edmund Dolbeare of Boston and Salem, Massachusetts, between 1671 and 1710. Another seventeenth-century English-type plate made here is the multiple-reed brim, a plate with brim of medium width having two to four rings near the edge. These are the most common of English seventeenth-century pewter items but only a few American examples exist. Such plates frequently have hallmark-type touch marks on the front of the brim and sometimes the owner's initials.

Smooth wide-brim dish with deep well. Narrow bead on underside of brim, hammered all over. Diameter: 15⅜ inches. One of the earliest surviving American dishes. Edmund Dolbeare, Boston and Salem, Massachusetts, 1671–c. 1710. (Courtesy of the Henry Francis du Pont Winterthur Museum)

Dish with multiple-reed brim. Diameter: 15 inches. Attributed to Joseph or John Dolbeare, Boston, 1694–1720. (Courtesy of the Henry Francis du Pont Winterthur Museum)

Above *Single-reed brim dish hammered all over. Simon Edgell, 1713–42. (The Metropolitan Museum of Art. Gift of Joseph France, 1943)* Above right *Smooth-brim plate. Frederick Bassett, 1761–99. (The Metropolitan Museum of Art. Gift of Joseph France, 1943)* Right *Single-reed deep dish. Skimming marks visible in photograph. Thomas Danforth III, 1777–1818. (The Metropolitan Museum of Art. Gift of Joseph France, 1943)*

Around 1700 the multiple-reed plate was simplified to a single reed, and this became the prevailing American-style plate with very few exceptions. For an interval from about 1740 to about 1790, a number of makers turned out smooth-brim plates, generally in the nine-inch size. During this period, the single-reed coexisted with the smooth-brim and continued on when the latter ceased to be made. In order to strengthen the plates the pewterers' company of London required that the booge be hammered (the curved side wall between bottom and brim) and from 1750 until the Revolution most American pewterers followed this custom. However, the generation starting work after the war abandoned the practice.

Since so many of the plates in existence here today are of English origin, it is useful to be able to quickly identify the most common. Probably more than half of these were made by the firm of John Townsend of London (1748–1817), which includes Townsend and Giffin, Townsend and Reynolds, Townsend and Compton, and Thomas and Townsend Compton. The London firm of Thomas Ellis and Thomas Swanson (1721–83) also sent vast quantities of pewter here. Other marks likely to be found are those of Richard King of London (1745–98) and the Bristol firms of Robert Bush and Company and its successors—Bush and Perkins; Curtiss and Company; Edgar, Curtiss and Company; and Edgar and Son.

Basins

Basins were used for serving stews, vegetables, and similar foods and are not the same vessels meant by our modern word "basin" but are probably closer to what is meant by our modern word "bowl." They were enormously useful and were made in a wide range of sizes from less than three inches in diameter to over ten. The shape of basins was essentially unchanged in England and America from the middle of the seventeenth century on. English basins were sometimes hammered but that was not the case here. The mark is usually in the bottom of the well.

Basin. Samuel Hamlin, 1777–1801, or son Samuel E. Hamlin, 1801–56. (The Metropolitan Museum of Art. Gift of Mrs. J. Insley Blair, 1939, in memory of J. Insley Blair)

Basin. Sylvester Griswold, Baltimore, 1820. (The Metropolitan Museum of Art. Gift of Mrs. J. Insley Blair, 1939, in memory of J. Insley Blair)

Posset Cups and Caudle Cups

Caudle and posset cups are small two-handled cups with covers which were used during the seventeenth century. Caudle is wine or other alcoholic beverage with the addition of sugar, spices, and crumbled bread. Posset is more like porridge, since it is made of bread or oat cakes mixed with beer and spices and curdled with the addition of wine and beer. The beautiful cups which were used for these mixtures are extremely rare and generally unmarked.

Tankards and Mugs

The covered tankard embodies all that is best in early American pewter—chaste simplicity of form and honest, sturdy execution with very little surface decoration. The forms are stable and substantial without heaviness or clumsiness. American styles were derived from the English but lagged behind and persisted long after being abandoned in England because Americans could not be so cavalier in discarding their molds. After the wealthy abandoned the use of pewter, the making of tankards declined. The new customers, ordinary folk, preferred mugs which were cheaper than the more elaborate tankards, and by the end of the eighteenth century mugs had largely replaced them.

Very early pewter tankards are more rare than silver ones, since the silver ones were more likely to be treasured while those of pewter were turned in to be recast when worn or damaged. If a seventeenth-century American pewter tankard exists, it would most likely resemble the flat-top silver one by Jeremiah Dummer ca. 1676. English tankards can often be dated fairly accurately by the designs of cover, handle, and thumb-

Silver tankard with flat top. Jeremiah Dummer, Boston, c. 1675. (The Metropolitan Museum of Art, Anonymous gift, 1934)

31

Pewter tankard, domed top, crenate lip. William Bradford, Jr., New York, N. Y., 1719–58. (The Metropolitan Museum of Art. Gift of Mrs. J. Insley Blair)

Pewter tankard, domed top, crenate lip, bud handle terminal. Height: 6⅝ inches. Bottom diameter: 5 inches. John Will, New York, N. Y., 1752–54. (The Metropolitan Museum of Art. Gift of Mrs. J. Insley Blair, 1939, in memory of J. Insley Blair)

Pewter tankard with flat top and crenate lip. Frederick Bassett, New York, N. Y., 1761–99. (The Metropolitan Museum of Art. Rogers Fund, 1939)

Silver tankard. George Fielding, c. 1700–1740. (The Metropolitan Museum of Art. Bequest of A. T. Clearwater)

Pewter tankard with flat top and crenate lip. Frederick Bassett, New York, N. Y., 1761–99. (The Metropolitan Museum of Art. Gift of Mrs. J. Insley Blair, 1940, in memory of J. Insley Blair)

piece, but this is not possible for American tankards. When a new type appeared in England, it was taken up in America only as an addition to the models currently being made and not as a replacement. Thus in American tankards there is a mixture of new contemporary features with those long out of date in England. Some flat-topped tankards exist by American makers who worked before the Revolution but most of them have left straight-sided tankards with double-domed lids (sometimes crenated), handles made with the slush molding process (hollow), and with scroll thumbpieces. Makers who spanned the Revolutionary years (roughly 1760–1800) have left flat-lidded tankards with projecting crenate lids and either scroll or open thumbpieces. The flat-lidded tankard with crenate lid was obsolete in England by 1720. In America, the tulip-shaped tankard had a brief period from about 1755 to about 1780 and they are extremely rare. The silver tankards set the styles for the pewter ones and several are shown in the illustrations.

After 1790 mugs, or pots, as they are termed in the early inventories, served the double purpose of drinking vessel and measure. Mugs, though scarce, are far more plentiful than tankards. The straight-sided shape was the principal type but a few tulip ones were made. In general, there was little change in the basic form throughout the period. The double-C handle came into vogue in England about 1750 and was used here on a few late tankards and some mugs. In the second half of the eighteenth century a solid straplike handle was made, much like the earlier one except that it was attached to the body by a strut. Later handles frequently have struts.

Silver tankard, tulip shape, domed lid. Jacob Geritten Lansing, c. 1750–75. (The Metropolitan Museum of Art. Bequest of A. T. Clearwater)

Pewter tankard, tulip shape, double-dome lid. William Will, Philadelphia, 1754–98. (The Metropolitan Museum of Art. Gift of Mrs. J. Insley Blair, 1939, in memory of J. Insley Blair)

Mug. Henry Will, 1761–93. (The Metropolitan Museum of Art. Gift of Mrs. J. Insley Blair, 1940, in memory of J. Insley Blair)

Mug. Nathaniel Austin, 1763–1807. (The Metropolitan Museum of Art. Gift of Mrs. J. Insley Blair, in memory of J. Insley Blair)

Quart mug. Thomas Danforth III, 1777–1818. (The Metropolitan Museum of Art. Gift of Joseph France, 1943)

Mug. Samuel Danforth of Hartford, 1795–1816. (The Metropolitan Museum of Art. Gift of Mrs. J. Insley Blair, in memory of J. Insley Blair)

Mug. Samuel Kilbourn, 1814–39. (The Metropolitan Museum of Art. Gift of Joseph France, 1943)

Barrel-shaped mug. Parks Boyd, 1795–1819. (The Metropolitan Museum of Art. Gift of Joseph France, 1943)

Mug. Height: 5¹³/₁₆ inches. T. D. & S. Boardman. 1810–50. (The Metropolitan Museum of Art. Gift of Dr. Georgiana Leffingwell, 1950)

Porringers

In the inventory of David Melville's shop in 1801, there are beer pint porringers, wine pint, jill, and half-jill porringers, or molds to make them. This clearly indicates that these were used for drinking and measuring alcoholic beverages. They probably found employment for soups and stews as well. The inventory of Richard Estabrook, pewterer and brazier, made in 1721 contained in addition to ordinary porringers "8 doz. & 9 Blood Porringers," so that some type also served in the widespread custom of bleeding.

Although porringers were used here very early, most of the surviving ones were made after 1800. In England porringers became obsolete by 1750, but Bristol continued to make them for export until about 1775. Marked English porringers are found here very rarely compared with those of American origin, quite the reverse of the situation with plates. Porringers were made in good numbers here until about 1825, mainly in New England, with the bulk of them coming from Rhode Island. Samuel Hamlin made more porringers than any other maker, outnumbering his plates by twenty to one.

There are two shapes of bowls, the standard and the basin. The standard shape has bulging sides, bottom with domed center surrounded by a flat ring-shaped gutter and a narrow collar around the top. The basin bowl is quite simply a basin with a handle attached and occurs generally in the small and large sizes. Porringers range from about two to about six inches in diameter. The two-inch size range is called a taster or wine-taster porringer, probably euphemistically, since a two-and-a-quarter-inch-diameter basin porringer holds precisely the same amount of fluid as a modern one-ounce whisky measure. Perhaps wine-tasting really was all the rage in Springfield, Vermont, in 1810 when the Richard Lees were making these small porringers.

The main feature of interest in porringers is the diversification in handle designs. Although there are a few rare instances where porringers have two or four handles, the usual porringer has one. The two main types may be classified as solid or openwork. The solid ones are simple,

COMMON TYPES OF PORRINGER HANDLES

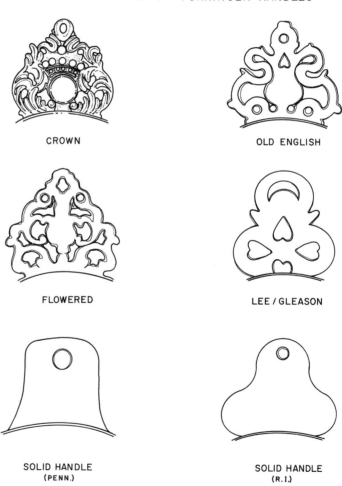

CROWN

OLD ENGLISH

FLOWERED

LEE / GLEASON

SOLID HANDLE
(PENN.)

SOLID HANDLE
(R.I.)

Porringer, basin bowl with solid tab handle. Pennsylvania type. Elisha Kirk, 1781–90. (The Metropolitan Museum of Art. Gift of Mrs. J. Insley Blair, 1941, in memory of J. Insley Blair)

Porringer with solid tab handle, Newport type. Samuel and Thomas Melville, 1793–1800. (The Metropolitan Museum of Art. Gift of Mrs. J. Insley Blair, 1941, in memory of J. Insley Blair)

unadorned tab handles with a hole for hanging on a nail or hook. This style derives from the Continent and is found in the country districts of Pennsylvania and in Newport, Rhode Island. The Newport handle differs in shape from the Pennsylvania handle in being less angular.

The openwork handles may be divided into four general types: flowered, crown, old English, and dolphin. Old English was the type most prevalent in England and is probably the most prevalent here. It occurs on small porringers and up to the twelve-fluid-ounce size. The flowered handle was especially popular in New England and was not made in New York or Pennsylvania. The crown handle, an English provincial design of Bristol origin, was an innovation of the pewterer and has no known silver prototype. The dolphin handle, also an English design, is by far the most rare handle type. All these basic types occur with variation, some of which are characteristic of the pewterer. Individualists like the Richard Lees made designs unique to them which fall outside of ready classification.

One of the most impenetrable pewter mysteries is that of the initialed porringers. These porringers, which appear to be of New England origin,

Porringer with Old English handle. T. D. & S. Boardman, 1810–30. (The Metropolitan Museum of Art. Gift of Mrs. J. Insley Blair, 1941, in memory of J. Insley Blair)

Porringer with flowered handle. Gershom Jones, 1774–1809. (The Metropolitan Museum of Art. Gift of Mrs. J. Insley Blair, 1941, in memory of J. Insley Blair)

Porringer with flowered handle. Samuel E. Hamlin, 1801–56. (The Metropolitan Museum of Art. Gift of Mrs. J. Insley Blair, 1941, in memory of J. Insley Blair)

Rare basin bowl porringer with dolphin handle. Diameter: 5⅝ inches. Depth: 2 inches. Unmarked. (Private collection)

Porringer with crown handle. Diameter: 5 inches. Unmarked. (Private collection)

Porringer with geometric handle. Joseph Belcher, Sr. or Jr., 1769–84. (The Metropolitan Museum of Art. Gift of Mrs. J. Insley Blair, 1941, in memory of J. Insley Blair)

Porringer. Richard Lee, Sr. or Jr., 1788–1820. (The Metropolitan Museum of Art. Gift of Mrs. J. Insley Blair, 1941, in memory of J. Insley Blair)

Porringer. Richard Lee, Sr. or Jr., 1788–1820. (The Metropolitan Museum of Art. Gift of Mrs. J. Insley Blair, 1941, in memory of J. Insley Blair)

Porringer, basin bowl. Diameter: 2⅞ inches. Richard Lee, Sr. or Jr., 1788–1820. (Private collection)

are marked by initials cast, not stamped, on the back of porringer handles or brackets. The initials are E. C. (or G.), S. G., I. G. (or C.), R. G., W. N., and C. P. At present there is no hard evidence to link the initials with known makers with the same initials. It is possible that the molds were bought from or handed down by an earlier maker with the new maker failing to remove the old initials. Perhaps some of these porringers were made in Bristol, England, specifically for export to America after they became obsolete there. Bristol had a reputation for sending some rather poorly finished articles here and some of these handles are rather crudely done. Crown-handled porringers with initials cast on the support brackets have appeared in England. However, the consensus among experts is overwhelmingly in favor of American origin, and especially behind Boston. Boston was an important pewter center, yet, inexplicably, no marked Boston porringers exist although they are listed in shop inventories. A rather good selection of initialed, unmarked, and marked porringers is available to the collector.

Teapots, sugar bowls, and creamers

The earliest silver teapot was made in England in 1670 and bears the arms of the East India Company. The earliest surviving American teapot is of silver, globular in form with a straight spout and large earlike handle, made ca. 1705. It is not known when the first pewter teapots were made here but the earliest surviving example is one by Francis Bassett, I or II, most likely pre-Revolutionary. It is ellipsoid rather than globular, and has a short curved spout. The next in point of time are teapots of the Revolutionary period, of Queen Anne design with pear-shaped body, high-domed lid, and large ear-shaped wooden handle. These follow the designs of the silver ones of the colonial period rather

Silver teapot, pear-shaped Queen Anne style. Jesse Kipp, New York, N. Y., c. 1720. (The Metropolitan Museum of Art. Gift of Mrs. Denise Barkalow, 1961)

Pewter teapot. Pear-shaped Queen Anne style with wood handle. William Kirby, New York, N. Y., 1760–93. (The Metropolitan Museum of Art. Gift of Mrs. J. Insley Blair, 1946, in memory of J. Insley Blair)

Silver teapot, part of a set. Cylindrical with straight spout. John Letelier, Philadelphia 1770–1800. (The Metropolitan Museum of Art. Gift of Mrs. J. Amory Haskell, in memory of the families of John L. Riker and Jonathan Amory Haskell, 1940)

Pewter teapot. Cylindrical with straight spout. William Will, Philadelphia, 1764–98. (The Metropolitan Museum of Art. Gift of Mrs. J. Insley Blair, 1940, in memory of J. Insley Blair)

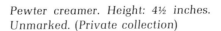

Pewter creamer. Height: 4½ inches. Unmarked. (Private collection)

Elegant Philadelphia Federal style silver coffee pot. Height: 14½ inches. Joseph Richardson, Jr. working 1777–c. 1805. This pot bears one of his early marks. (Collection Chatham R. Wheat III. Courtesy R. T. Trump & Co., Inc.)

Pewter coffee pot in same superb Philadelphia style. The decorative rings of beading are strikingly similar to the Richardson pot. Height: 15¾ inches. William Will, 1764–98. (Courtesy of the Henry Francis du Pont Winterthur Museum)

Philadelphia sugar bowl with cover. Height: 4⅝ inches. Unmarked. Attributed to William Will, 1765–90. (The Metropolitan Museum of Art. Rogers Fund, 1947)

Covered sugar bowl. Thomas Danforth III, 1777–1818. (The Metropolitan Museum of Art. Gift of Mrs. J. Insley Blair, 1941, in memory of J. Insley Blair)

closely. Little pot-bellied cream jugs were made to accompany these and are frequently unmarked. These early teapots are even rarer than the contemporary tankards.

During the Federal period, tea and coffee pots assumed new forms. The coffee pot became tall and imposing with urn-shaped body, elongated neck and spout, and high-domed lid. The use of rolled sheet silver resulted in short, oval, cylindrical teapots made of sheet silver and seamed. Sugar bowls, creamers, and tea caddies were made from sheets in the same way. These forms were copied by the early brittania workers such as George Coldwell, Philip Lee, Israel Trask, and Eben Smith using sheet metal in the early decades of the nineteenth century. Decorative engraving was copied from the silversmith as well as the method of fabrication.

Tankard and beakers, both part of a communion service from a church in Jaffrey, New Hampshire. Tankard height: 7⅛ inches. Unmarked. Beaker height: 5⅛ inches. Edward Danforth, 1786–95. (Courtesy of the Brooklyn Museum)

Ecclesiastical Pewter

The American colonies followed the European custom of using pewter communion services in the poorer churches. There is no clearcut distinction between household pewter and that for ecclesiastical use. Often a tankard or a beaker was presented to a church as a gift by an individual. Rarely did a church have a matched set purchased all at one time. Its pieces were assembled over a period of time and the number varied with the size and affluence of the congregation. Basic items were at least one flagon for pouring wine; two or more drinking vessels in the form of beakers, chalices, or church cups; one or more moderately large dishes; and a basin or bowl for baptism. Sometimes six-inch plates were used for patens.

Flagons are one of the most imposing forms in American pewter. Unfortunately, no marked example is known which was made before 1750. Marked flagons made before 1790 are very rare and fall into two distinct types; the William Will type, which resembles a tall elongated tankard and has no spout in its earliest form, and the Lancaster, Pensylvania, type. The Lancaster flagons by Christopher Heyne are derived from Germanic designs rather than English. They are tall with flaring base set on cherub-head medallions for feet.

Between 1790 and 1825, two other types of flagons were made: the Albany and the Boardman. The Albany ones were made by Spencer

Flagon, two-quart. T. D. & S. Boardman,
1810–30. (The Metropolitan Museum of Art.
Gift of Joseph France, 1943)

Chalice. John Christopher Heyne, 1742–80.
(The Metropolitan Museum of Art. Gift of
Joseph France, 1943)

Stafford and Timothy Bridgen and became the prototype for a widely made and common type of coffee pot. The Boardmans usually made handsome, dignified vessels.

Church cups, chalices, and beakers are rarely marked. Identification of them is by comparison with items whose maker is known, by comparison of parts with parts by known makers, and by association with flagons whose maker is known. Pewter chalices and church cups are as graceful as their silver counterparts. Tall and short beakers occur marked and unmarked, the unmarked being far less expensive and more available to the collector.

The first baptismal bowls were probably basins. Later, a foot was added to an ordinary basin, and then footed bowls were made. These are generally appealing to the eye.

Chalice. Height: 8⅞ inches. Timothy Brigden, 1804–19. (The Metropolitan Museum of Art. Gift of Joseph France, 1943)

Two-handled church cup made from a beaker. Height: 5½ inches. T. D. & S. Boardman, 1810–30. (The Metropolitan Museum of Art. Gift of Joseph France)

Beaker. Samuel Danforth of Hartford, 1795–1816. (The Metropolitan Museum of Art. Gift of Mrs. J. Insley Blair, 1941, in memory of J. Insley Blair)

Beaker. Height: 3½ inches. Timothy Boardman & Co., 1822–25. (Private collection)

Beaker with flared lip. T. D. & S. Boardman, 1810–30. (The Metropolitan Museum of Art. Gift of Mrs. J. Insley Blair)

Baptismal bowl formed from two eight-inch basins. Height: 3½ inches. Samuel Danforth of Hartford, 1795–1816. (Courtesy of the Brooklyn Museum)

Baptismal bowl. Robert Palethorp, Jr., 1817–21. (The Metropolitan Museum of Art. Gift of Mrs. J. Insley Blair, 1940, in memory of J. Insley Blair)

Miscellaneous

Many of the items so frequently mentioned in the early inventories are now exceedingly rare. As they became obsolete, they were probably melted down in order to recycle the metal. Babies' bottles, which were part of nearly every household, were replaced by glass when it became readily available. Chamber pots were not treasured for obvious reasons although of handsome form. Some of the other objects made of pewter were buttons; buckles; furniture knob pulls; small picture frames; fifes; medals; boxes for soap, tinder, tea, and spices; dram bottles; and bedwarming pans. Robert Boyle advertised doll dishes, plates, and platters in New York in 1781. Miniatures, though charming, are expensive, hard to find, and seldom marked.

A large number of spoon molds exist, so that many spoons must have been made, although very few have been found. The earliest marked American pewter object discovered here is a spoon excavated near Jamestown, Virginia. Ladles, which are sturdier, are found somewhat more often.

Button with eagle and "Massachusetts, 1787." Eighteenth century. (The Metropolitan Museum of Art. Gift of Robert M. Parmelee and Mrs. William M. Parker, 1916)

Set of four miniature frames enclosing silhouettes of a family group from Newfane, Vermont. Attributed to Richard Lee, Sr. or Jr., c. 1810. (Private collection)

Rare pattern bar for embossing designs on cookies or butter.

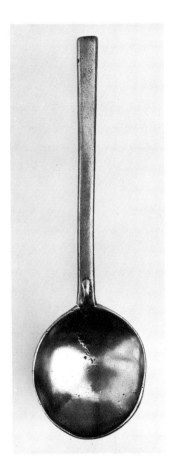

Spoon with handle decorated with flags and motto "Peace & America." Length: 7⅜ inches. George Coldwell, 1787–1811. (The Metropolitan Museum of Art. Gift of Mrs. J. Insley Blair, 1941, in memory of J. Insley Blair)

Spoon with round bowl. Length: 7⅛ inches. William Ellsworth, 1776–98. (The Metropolitan Museum of Art. Gift of Mrs. J. Insley Blair, 1941, in memory of J. Insley Blair)

Spoon with floral motif on handle. Length: 4¾ inches. Richard Lee, Sr. or Jr., 1788–1820. (The Metropolitan Museum of Art. Gift of Mrs. J. Insley Blair, 1941, in memory of J. Insley Blair)

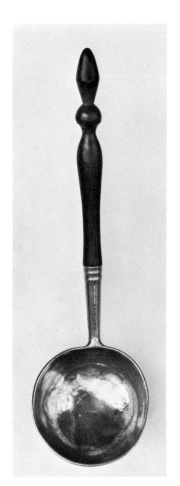

Ladle with wood handle. Richard Lee, Sr. or Jr., 1788–1820. (The Metropolitan Museum of Art. Gift of Mrs. J. Insley Blair, 1941, in memory of J. Insley Blair)

Shaker with stopper in the base. Thomas Danforth III, 1777–1818. (The Metropolitan Museum of Art. Gift of Joseph France, 1943)

Since the makers' marks on pewter objects can be used to identify when, where, and by whom it was made, marked pieces are vital to historical reconstruction and help to identify unmarked pieces. The first recorded American pewterer is Richard Graves, who came to this country in 1635 and settled in Salem, Massachusetts. No examples of his work are known.

A brief biography is given below for some individual pewterers of special interest to collectors. The dates next to the names are the approximate working dates.

Nathanial Austin (1763–1807)

Austin established himself as a pewterer in Charlestown, Massachusetts, in 1763. After the British shelled Charlestown, he moved to Lunenberg, returning to rebuild his shop around 1780. His surviving output consists of a full range of plates and dishes, with both smooth and normal brims, basins and quart mugs.

Richard Austin (ca. 1793–1807)

Austin opened his first shop in Boston about 1792. In 1810 he entered some speculative real estate ventures with a fellow member of the artillery company. A sudden collapse of the enterprise forced Austin to return to pewtering. His marks exist on a wide range of plates and on eight-inch basins.

Thomas Badger, Jr. (1787–1815)

Badger entered the pewtering business in Boston around 1786. He joined the militia and in 1813 rose to the rank of colonel and also served on numerous civic committees. Only eight-inch basins and a wide range of plates have been found with his mark.

Blak(e)slee Barn(e)s (1812–17)

Barns was born in Wallingford, Connecticut, in 1781. He was apprenticed to a tinsmith and opened a small shop in Berlin, Connecticut. In 1809 he went to Philadelphia and opened a pewtering shop a few doors from that of Thomas Danforth III. In five years he built up one of the largest pewter trades in the country, then sold out and moved back to Berlin, where he died in 1823. Apparently, he made only plates and basins. His plates are readily available to the collector.

The Bassetts (1718–99)

The Bassetts, and Frederick in particular, dominated the pewter trade in New York City. Francis I was born in New York in 1690 and was apprenticed to a pewterer in 1707. His first cousin, John, who was about six years younger, also became a pewterer as did two of John's sons, Francis II (b. 1729) and Frederick (b. ca. 1740). Francis II was appointed to the General Committee of Safety for the City and County of New York at the start of the Revolution and was active in various civic posts. Few pieces of his pewter survive and there is much confusion between his work and that of his father, John, and his cousin, Francis I. Frederick's pewter is more plentiful than any other contemporary New York maker. He is especially noted for his superb flat-topped tankards but he also made plates, basins, mugs, porringers, beakers, funnels, nursing bottles, and commodes. Except for several years, 1781–86, when he lived in Hartford, Connecticut, Frederick worked in New York until he died in 1800.

Parks Boyd (1795–1819)

Boyd was born in Philadelphia in 1771 or 1772 and spent his life there working at pewtering and brass founding. He made the usual plates and dishes, pint and quart mugs, but also some rather unusual barrel-shaped mugs, tall covered pitchers, and quart tankards.

The Danforths

The Danforths produced pewterers for five generations and dominated pewter making in Connecticut. Their influence extended beyond the boundaries of the state with their aggressive merchandizing which sent peddlers with their carts of pewter all over the East. For the period 1775–90 more Connecticut pewter exists than that of all the other states together.

John Danforth (1773–93)

John was born in Norwich, Connecticut, in 1741, the fifth child of Thomas Danforth I. He worked in his father's shop in Norwich until 1773 when their partnership was dissolved and continued on his own for another twenty years or so. His son, Samuel of Norwich (b. 1772–d. 1827), continued the business until 1803 but his pewter is exceedingly scarce.

Joseph Danforth I (1780–88) and Joseph Danforth II (1807–12)

Joseph I, the second son of Thomas Danforth II, was a pewterer in Middletown until his death at the age of thirty. His younger brothers, Jonathan and William, continued the business. Joseph's son, Joseph II, became a pewterer and moved to Richmond, Virginia, about 1805.

Samuel Danforth (1795–1816) of Hartford

Samuel Danforth of Hartford was the youngest son of Thomas II. He was making pewter by 1795 and has left a large variety, all marked with eagles.

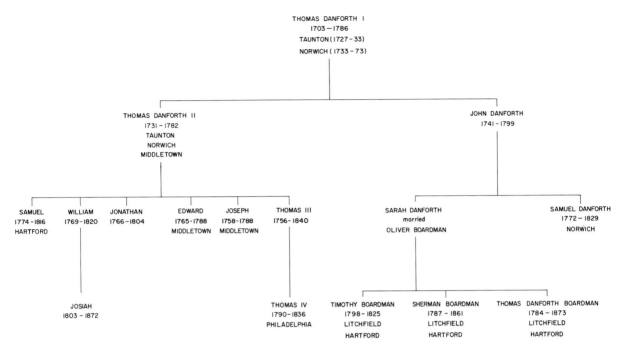

Family chart of the remarkable Danforth and Boardman pewterers.

Thomas III, the eldest son of Thomas II, opened his shop in Stepney (Rock Hill) in 1777. In 1807 he opened a second shop in Philadelphia and in 1813 moved back to Stepney.

Samuel Hamlin (ca. 1768–1801) and Samuel E. Hamlin (1801–56)

Samuel Hamlin began his career in Middletown, Connecticut, as a partner of Thomas Danforth II. He then moved to Providence some time in 1773 and opened his own shop. During the years 1774–81 he was in partnership with his brother-in-law Gershom Jones. His career was interrupted by service in the First Rhode Island Regiment during the Revolution. His son, Samuel Ely Hamlin, born in 1774, worked in his father's shop and after his death continued the business. As with most such cases it is difficult to distinguish the work of the father from that of the son. Hamlin porringers are found more frequently than any other marked American porringers, and outnumber marked Hamlin plates. They marked their plates in the well rather than on the bottom. Samuel E. died in 1864, spanning most of the brittania period.

Johann Christopher Heyne (1742–80)

Heyne was born in Saxony in 1715 and migrated to Philadelphia with a group of Moravians in 1742, eventually settling in Lancaster as a pewterer. His work shows a remarkable progression from Germanic line and detail to that of English. The flagons demonstrate this stylistic adaptation most markedly. Heyne's chalices are superb.

Gershom Jones (1774–1809)

Jones was trained in Norwich, Connecticut, and in 1751 at the age of twenty-one moved to Providence, Rhode Island. In 1774 he became a partner with his brother-in-law, Samuel Hamlin. Jones served in the Continental Army and in 1790 achieved the rank of major in the Providence United Train of Artillery. The partnership was dissolved and in 1784 Jones opened his own shop. Existing items are porringers, plates, and mugs.

Richard Lee, Sr. (1788–1820), and Jr. (1795–1816)

Richard, Sr., was born in Scituate, Rhode Island. He led a wandering existence except for service in the army beginning in 1775 and eventually settled in Springfield, Vermont, in 1802. Richard, Jr., was born in Rehoboth, Massachusetts, in 1775 and settled in Springfield, Vermont, in 1795. The Lees are noted for their porringers, with original and sometimes whimsical handle designs which are highly prized by collectors.

The Melvilles (1776–1824)

David Melville was born in Newport in 1755. His pewtering career was interrupted by service in the Rhode Island Regiment during the Revolution and ended with his early death in 1793. His two younger brothers, Samuel and Thomas, carried on his business using many of his touches until David Melville's son Thomas II (b. 1779) took over his father's business in 1796. Porringers, with plain and flowered handles, basins, and plates are typical products.

The Palethorps (1817–45)

Robert Palethorp, Jr., opened a shop in Philadelphia in 1817. After Boyd's death he bought out the contents of his shop. In 1820, his younger brother, John Harrison Palethorp, became his partner. Robert Palethorp, Jr., died in 1822 when only twenty-five. Robert, Sr., although not trained as a pewterer, then took over his deceased son's interest until his own death in 1825. His other son, John, continued working well into the brittania period.

Semper Eadem (before 1770 to ca. 1790)

The actual identity of the Boston pewterer or pewterers who used Semper Eadem in his rose-and-crown touch is still a mystery. This is the most frequently found of Boston pre-Revolutionary marks and is found on a wide range of plates, dishes, and basins.

John Skinner (1760–90)

Skinner was born in Marblehead in 1733 and was well established as a pewterer in Boston by 1761. His identifiable work includes normal-brim and smooth-brim plates, mostly hammered, basins, but no hollowware, although he is known to have made some.

John Will (1752–74) and **Henry Will** (1761–75, 1783–93)

Both Henry Will and his father, John, were born in Germany and migrated to New York City in 1752. The pair were talented pewterers and are noted for their flat-topped Stuart-type tankards. They made some forms unusual for American workers such as hot-water plates, foot-warmers, and double-lidded inkstands as well as plates, dishes, and mugs.

William Will (1764–98)

William Will is the Paul Revere of American pewter—patriot, soldier, and outstanding craftsman. He was born in the Rhineland in 1742 and came to this country in 1752 when his father John migrated to New York. The Will family was a family of pewterers, father John Will, brother Henry, and brother Philip. William made his home in Philadelphia and was established there as a pewterer by 1772. In 1776, he organized a company of infantry called "Captain Will's Company of Associators." In 1777, he became lieutenant-colonel of the First Battalion and served afterward as an officer in other posts during the Revolution. He held many positions of trust and responsibility, was elected as sheriff of the city and county of Philadelphia and as representative to the General Assembly in Philadelphia in 1785.

His pewter is noted for its fine workmanship and originality. His coffee and teapots are among the most elegant surviving American examples and his flagons are without parallel. His shop inventory lists a wide range of forms. Numerous items, although unmarked, have been attributed to him with considerable assurance by identifying them as having come from a Colonel William Will mold.

4

Second Period 1825–1860

This Second Period, often called the Brittania Period, is not so much characterized by a change in the pewter alloy but by the methods by which it was fabricated. Brittania was made in America early in the nineteenth century but did not come into widespread use until the application of spinning and stamping machines which required the new hard alloy for success. These new methods made possible a flexible response to a changing market, no longer that mainly of the dinner plate but of coffee pots and teapots. Fine and handsome objects were made both by workers who began in the First Period and adapted to the new and by new men who entered the field. This is the period in which the collector will find the largest number and variety of objects available to him. The collector who neglects these might remember the Duke of Urbino, who collected only handwritten manuscripts, scorning the Gutenberg Bible and other incunabula as mechanical products.

Tea and Coffee Pots

Coffee pots and teapots replaced plates as the bulk of the pewterer's trade by 1825 and survive in larger numbers than any other form. William Calder's records from 1826 to 1838 show that his most popular items during these years were teapots. The distinction between tea and coffee pots is not clear and cannot be determined by size alone. Calder's sales records for 1826 to 1838 tell us that the larger teapots became increasingly popular during these years. In 1826, his best seller was a quart-sized teapot, but by 1838 the two-quart size was the frontrunner. The tall pots also have strainers at the base of the spout just like the smaller ones universally accepted as teapots.

Federal style teapot with straight spout and wood handle. Height: 6¼ inches. Greatest width: 10 inches. Israel Trask, c. 1813–25. (The Metropolitan Museum of Art. Gift of Mrs. Stephen S. FitzGerald, 1962)

Teapots were made of brittania long before 1825. Thomas Danforth Boardman started making cast pots of brittania about 1807. In New York, George Coldwell was using the seaming method with brittania some time prior to 1811. In Beverly, Massachusetts, the seaming method for making teapots from sheets of brittania was used by a group of workers beginning with Lee and Creesy around 1807. It is not known whether Philip Lee brought the formula from Great Britain with him or whether he and his partner developed it here. In any case, their work is a break with the past because they applied silversmithing techniques instead of following the traditional casting procedure.

The early teapots made by the Beverly Group were those readily formed from flat sheets of metal. The first of these styles is a small oval

Federal style teapot with decorative engraving, curved spout, ball feet. Height: 6⅞ inches. Israel Trask, c. 1813–25. (Courtesy of the Currier Gallery of Art)

Silver chocolate pot. Truncated cone body with domed lid adapted for pewter tea and coffee pots. Height: 9⅞ inches. Zachariah Brigden, c. 1760–90. (Museum of Fine Arts, Boston. The Misses Rose and Elizabeth Townsend)

True classic form. Lighthouse teapot with decorative engraving. Height: 11¾ inches. Eben Smith, c. 1814–30. (Courtesy of the Brooklyn Museum of Art. Dick S. Ramsay Fund)

cylindrical Federal pot with ball feet made by Lee and Creesy. Their successor, Israel Trask, made this style also, frequently with bands of decorative engraving. Initially, these pots were made with wooden handles provided by Eben Smith, who had been trained as a cabinet-maker, but later ones had cast metal handles painted black to resemble wood.

The seaming method was also used to make the lighthouse pot and its variations which derive from an eighteenth-century silver form. This type of pot in silver was most frequently a coffee or chocolate pot. The bodies of these pewter pots are truncated cones sometimes flaring out near the base. Their special feature is the high-domed lid which was made in variations with stepped domes. The Beverly Group led in the making of these pots, usually with bands of decorative engraving. Attractive as Israel Trask's lighthouse pots are, they are thin-walled and

Lighthouse tea or coffee pot, cast. Height: 11 inches. William Calder, Providence, Rhode Island, 1817–56. (Private collection)

Lighthouse pot, cast. Height: 10¼ inches. Charles Yale, Wallingford, Connecticut, 1817–35. (Courtesy of the International Silver Company)

Lighthouse pot, cast. Height: 11 inches. Roswell Gleason, Dorchester, Massachusetts, c. 1830–35. (Private collection)

Lighthouse pot, cast. Height: 10 inches. Reed & Barton, Taunton, Massachusetts, c. 1840–50.

easily dented. The style was quite popular since it was made by many other makers, most of them using the casting method. Handsome cast lighthouse pots were made by William Calder, George Richardson, and Roswell Gleason among others. They are from ten to twelve inches in height and hold one and a half to two quarts easily.

Judging by the number of makers who produced it, the elongated pear shape was one of the most popular styles of tall pots until about 1840. It is also derived from an eighteenth-century silver coffee or chocolate pot form. The pewter pots are fuller bellied and have cast or incised rings around the body but like the earlier silver ones have high double-domed lids, and are set on a circular base. The handle shapes of the pewter pots vary somewhat and are usually made of metal which is painted black to resemble wood. The flat disk finials are made of wood, bone, composition, or pewter. The pewter alloy of the cast handles and spouts differs from that of the body, as soon becomes painfully clear to anyone who tries to clean a badly corroded pot. These large bulbous pots are around twelve inches tall and hold two and a half quarts easily. Some were spun and some were cast. Thomas D. & Sherman Boardman, George Richardson, Ashbil Griswold, Josiah Danforth, Savage and Graham, and Allen Porter were among the makers who produced this type.

Silver coffeepot, elongated pear shape. Height: 13½ inches. Paul Revere, 1773. (Worcestor Art Museum. Gift of Francis Thomas and Eliza Sturgis Paine in memory of Frederick William Paine)

Pewter teapot, elongated pear shape, spun. Height: 11⅛ inches. S. Simpson 1835–52. (Courtesy of the International Silver Company)

Other styles of tall pots were made using the spinning process and exhibit the broken outline caused by the juxtaposition of shapes made with different chucks or different techniques. The Richardson pot illustrated is a pastiche with one of his sugar bowls for the lower part of the body, and the dome of the lid from another pot. Griswold's records show that in 1828 he bought teapot tops from Howard Pratt & Co., which he in turn sold to Josiah Danforth by the gross. Many teapot lids were made by the stamping process and possibly pewterers bought such parts from shops with this new and specialized equipment. If this practice was widespread, it might give pause to too facile identification of an unmarked piece on the basis of an identical part.

The many short pots made by these methods are examples of pure nineteenth-century design, a product of their time. Considerable ingenuity is shown in constructing new forms from separate parts, often made using different techniques, and are unlike anything made before. Some have broken outlines and some smooth curves. The most distinctive and original pots of the period were made in Connecticut, where a special flair was added with its cusped lid. These are not copies of silver models but are indigenous pewter designs.

Teapot with lower part made for sugar, bowl by same maker. George Richardson, 1818–45. (The Metropolitan Museum of Art. Rogers Fund, 1939)

Tea or coffee pot. Height: 10½ inches. Boardman and Hart, 1827–47. (Courtesy of the Henry Francis du Pont Winterthur Museum)

Group of three teapots. Left: Unmarked. Center: H. B. Ward & Co., Wallingford, Connecticut, c. 1849. Right: S. Simpson, Yalesville, Connecticut, 1837–52.

Teapot, spun. Height: 7⅜ inches. Ashbil Griswold, Meriden, Connecticut, 1807–35. (Courtesy of the International Silver Company)

Teapot, spun. Height: 7¼ inches. Allen Porter, Westbrook, Maine, 1830–38. (Private collection)

Teapot, spun. Height: 9⅝ inches. L. J. Curtiss, Meriden, Connecticut, 1836–52. (Courtesy of the International Silver Company)

Teapot. Height: 7¾ inches. William Calder, c. 1817–25. (Private collection)

Teapot. Height: 7½ inches. Josiah Danforth, 1821–43. (Private collection)

Teapot. Height: 7½ inches. R. Dunham, 1837–60. (Private collection)

Small teapot. Height: 5½ inches. T. D. & S. Boardman, 1810–30.

Connecticut teapot with cusp lid. Height: 8½ inches. Isaac C. Lewis, Meriden, Connecticut, 1834–50. (Private collection)

Connecticut teapot with cusp lid. Height: 9 inches. Lemuel J. Curtiss, Meriden, Connecticut, 1836–52.

Connecticut teapot with cusp lid. Morris Benham, West Meriden, Connecticut, 1849. (Courtesy of the International Silver Company)

A number of very attractive revival styles were made which are favorites of collectors. Variations of the short, squatty Queen Anne style teapots were made by Eben Smith, Roswell Gleason, the Boardmans, George Richardson, and J. B. Woodbury. A footed model was made by Samuel Danforth and Thomas D. Boardman which is somewhat taller. The eighteenth-century globular teapot was made in several versions.

Some styles followed the contemporary silver trends very closely, and some the English brittania styles of the Dixon Company. An example of the latter is a pigeon-breasted pot made of facets which are soldered together made by Roswell Gleason and Leonard, Reed, and Barton. Roswell Gleason and Israel Trask made a smooth pigeon-breasted pot as well. A distinctive form of the period is the impressive coffee urn by Roswell Gleason. As the Victorian period wore on, silver styles became ever more ornate. Pewter never reached the decorative excesses of silver, but did succumb to melon-shaped bodies and drooping finials.

Teapots, Queen Anne revival style. Heights: 7⅜ inches and 6⅞ inches. Both George Richardson, 1818–28. (Collection of Mrs. Rhoda Shaw Clark. Courtesy of the Currier Gallery of Art)

Pigeon-breasted teapot with facted body. Height: 10 inches. Leonard, Reed, and Barton, 1835–40. (Private collection)

Coffee urn. Height: 14 inches. Roswell Gleason. (Courtesy of the Brooklyn Museum)

Sugar Bowls and Creamers

Sugar bowls and creamers were made in far lesser numbers to accompany the tea and coffee pots. In 1830, Crossman, West, and Leonard made nearly four times as many tea and coffee pots as sugar and cream sets. The New York firm of Boardman and Hart made a matching pair in high empire style with a variation of the Connecticut cusped lid. It is a rhythmic and strong harmonious design.

Single sugar bowls exist by a number of makers. The sugar bowl by Ashbil Griswold shows clearly the component parts of which it is made, a characteristic of many items of this time. The much admired Richardson sugar bowl with the domed cover was made famous by appearing on the frontispiece of Kerfoot's pioneering book on American pewter written in 1924. It is universally appealing and testifies to the fact that fine objects were indeed made in the nineteenth century. Even more noteworthy is his sugar bowl with the hinged flap lid. It is so familiar looking as the prototype for the ubiquitous bowl on lunchroom tables and counters that one is apt to overlook it as a remarkable forerunner of the twentieth century. It could be a present-day design, being functional, streamlined, unornamented, and adaptable to mass production.

Covered sugar bowl and creamer. Height of sugar bowl: 8½ inches. Boardman & Hart, 1828–53. (Private collection)

Covered sugar bowl. Ashbil Griswol, 1807–35. (Courtesy of the International Silver Company)

Covered sugar bowl, Federal style with bright-cut engraving. Height: 7 inches. Unmarked, attributed to the Beverly Group. (Currier Gallery of Art)

Covered sugar bowl. Height: 5⅛ inches. The model used as the frontispiece in Kerfoot's book. George Richardson, 1828–48. (The Metropolitan Museum of Art. Rogers Fund, 1958)

Covered sugar bowl. Height: 4¾ inches. Lunchroom model. Remarkably modern looking for the second quarter of the nineteenth century. George Richardson, 1828–48. (The Metropolitan Museum of Art. Gift of Mrs. Stephen S. FitzGerald, 1962)

Pitchers

The nineteenth century was an age of barrels and kegs. Pitchers were enormously useful for bringing liquids to the table from the bulk storage areas. The two-quart open pitcher is often called a cider pitcher while the covered one is termed a beer pitcher. Since not every home had fresh water with the turn of a tap, they were probably also used for bringing water from the well or kitchen pump. Pitchers are among the most handsome of the contemporary forms. Open ones were made by Freeman Porter, the Boardmans, Rufus Dunham, McQuilken, and others. These resemble the china and pottery pitchers rather than the silver ones of the first half of the nineteenth century. The covered pitchers are of special merit and were made in a wide range of sizes from the monster one by Roswell Gleason to the small one by T. Sage. Covered pitchers were often used in church services in place of flagons.

Largest and smallest known covered pitchers. Heights: 12 inches and 5⅝ inches. Roswell Gleason, c. 1821–50, and Timothy Sage, 1847–48. (Private collection)

Open pitcher. Height: 6⅜ inches.
Freeman Porter, 1835–60. (Private
collection)

Lidded syrup pitchers. Heights: 6⅜ inches and 6¼ inches. Base diameters: 3⅜ inches and 4⅛ inches.
Sellew & Co., Cincinnati, Ohio, 1830–60, and William Savage, Middletown, Connecticut, late 1830's.
(Private collection)

Beakers and Tumblers

Beakers and tumblers were made in substantial numbers with Calder's Daybook for 1838 recording more of them sold than teapots. They were used for drinking in the home as well as communion cups in church. Sizes range from about one to six inches in height. Ashbil Griswold made a short one with flaring top and decorative incised rings. The tall slender one illustrated, by Oliver Trask, has decorative engraving between pairs of incised rings forming a pleasing and rhythmic pattern. Large numbers of beakers are in existence but only a few are marked.

Beaker. Ashbil Griswold, 1807–35. (The Metropolitan Museum of Art. Gift of Mrs. J. Insley Blair, 1941, in memory of J. Insley Blair)

Beaker. Oliver Trask, 1822–39. (The Metropolitan Museum of Art. Gift of Mrs. J. Insley Blair, 1941, in memory of J. Insley Blair)

Most existing pewter candlesticks were made during this period and are largely contemporary with the whale oil lamps. A vase-form stem was made by Henry Hopper, who occasionally embellished his with decorative engraving. Sellew and Co. produced an eight-inch stick with a baluster shaft and a domed base. Inventiveness is evident in the variety of knobs and turnings on the sticks by Gleason, Porter, and Rufus Dunham. The length was frequently extended by the repetition of one of the design elements. Short chamber sticks were made with saucer bases and ring handles of which Henry Hopper and Roswell Gleason have left marked examples. Lewis and Cowles made an unusual chamber stick with a push-up which occurs both marked and unmarked. Almost without exception these pewter candlesticks are appealing to the modern eye. Marked American candlesticks are rather scarce and sought after for their utility and attractiveness.

Candlestick. Height: 10 inches. Henry Hopper, 1842–47. (Private collection)

Candlestick. Height: 8 inches. Sellew & Co., 1832–60. (The Metropolitan Museum of Art. Gift of Mrs. Stephen S. FitzGerald, 1962)

Candlestick. Height: 7 inches. Roswell Gleason, c. 1821–50. (Currier Gallery of Art)

Candlestick. Height: 8 inches. Rufus Dunham, 1837–60. (Private collection)

Chamber stick with saucer base, ring handle. Height: 5⅛ inches. Henry Hopper, 1842–47. (The Metropolitan Museum of Art. Gift of Mrs. J. Insley Blair, 1941, in memory of J. Insley Blair)

Chamber stick with push-up, saucer base with ring handle. Unmarked. Attributed to Lewis and Cowles, c. 1835. (Private collection)

Lamps

The whale oil lamp was a new item, a "modern" development, which had no counterpart in the old period. They were made with the same bases as candlesticks by some makers. The next chapter will deal with whale oil lamps separately.

Cruet or Caster Frames

In the late 1830's cruet frames became an essential part of the dining table setting. Most of them have room for five bottles containing pepper, mustard, vinegar, oil, and hot sauce. Sometimes a salt was substituted for one of the cruets. In the more common types bottles hang from rings, while in others they stand on a platform with the rings to steady them. Rufus Dunham, Roswell Gleason, Israel Trask, and William Calder are known to have made them. In 1830, Crossman, West, and Leonard made no caster frames, but by 1838, the successor company of Leonard, Reed, and Barton made almost three times as many as they made teapots.

Cruet set, silverplated. Height: 13½ inches. Roswell Gleason, c. 1830–60. (Currier Gallery of Art. Gift of Miss L. Frances Sanborn)

The expansion of the church into the many poor frontier communities brought about a sizable demand for pewter accessories. The Boardmans continued making their handsome flagons and were joined by later makers such as Gleason. The Beverly Group made some with the seaming method as they did some chalices and beakers. In general, chalices are simple and graceful but rarely marked. They vary from straight-sided to tulip shape. Calder first mentions flagons and church cups as part of his output in 1830, christening bowls in 1834, communion basins in 1837, and ten- and twelve-inch plates in 1838. Christening basins varied from ordinary basins to the footed bowls made by Leonard, Reed, and Barton.

Flagon. Height: 12¾ inches. T. D. & S. Boardman, c. 1810–30. (Courtesy of the Henry Francis du Pont Winterthur Museum as shown in "Brittania in America" by Nancy Goyne, Winterthur Portfolio II)

Flagon. Height: 10½ inches. Boardman & Co., New York, 1825–27. (Private collection)

Flagon. Height: 10⅝ inches. Eben Smith, 1814–56. (Courtesy of the Currier Gallery of Art)

Flagon. Height: 11¼ inches. Israel Trask, 1813–56. (Courtesy of the Currier Gallery of Art)

Communion set. Flagon height: 10¼ inches. Unmarked. Height of chalices: 6⅛ inches. William Calder, 1817–56. Plate diameter: 10⅝ inches. William Calder, 1817–56. (Courtesy of the Currier Gallery of Art)

Communion set. Flagon height: 9¹³⁄₁₆ inches. Roswell Gleason, c. 1821–50. Height of chalices: 6⁷⁄₁₆ inches. Unmarked. Plate diameter: 10⅞ inches. Roswell Gleason. (Collection of Mrs. Edward B. Stearns. Courtesy the Currier Gallery of Art)

Pair of chalices and communion plate. Height of chalices: 6 inches. Plate diameter: 10½ inches. Both by Leonard, Reed, and Barton, 1835–40. (Currier Gallery of Art. Gift of Mrs. Frederick H. Curtis, 1963)

Chalice. Height: 5¾ inches. Israel Trask, 1813–56. (The Metropolitan Museum of Art. Gift of Mrs. Stephen S. FitzGerald, 1962)

Baptismal bowl. Height: 5¼ inches. Oliver Trask, 1832–39. (Collection of Mrs. Amos Kingsbury. Courtesy of the Currier Gallery of Art)

Baptismal bowl. Height: 5⅞ inches. Leonard, Reed, and Barton, 1837–40. (Courtesy of the Henry Francis du Pont Winterthur Museum as shown in "Brittania in America" by Nancy Goyne, Winterthur Portfolio II)

Other Forms

Some of the old forms continued to be made well into this period but lost their earlier importance. One of these was porringers which were made in decreasing numbers. They constituted thirteen per cent of Calder's output in 1826 with this percentage diminishing each year thereafter. Mugs also continued to be made, changing their forms only slightly from earlier times. Many miscellaneous forms were made such as boxes for snuff, soap, and shaving; cuspidors; silhouette frames; coffin plates; soup ladles; spoons; and toys. The thriving Roswell Gleason alone made plates, cuspidors, wash basins with handles, tea and coffee pots of various sizes, flagons, chalices, baptismal bowls, coffee urns, beakers, covered syrup pitchers, covered water pitchers, cruet sets, sugar bowls, creamers, spoons, ladles, porringers, mugs, tankards with screw-on tops, candlesticks, lamps, bedpans, cigar lighters, and shaving mugs.

Mug. Daniel Curtiss, 1822–40. (The Metropolitan Museum of Art. Gift of Joseph France, 1943)

Covered basin. Height: 8 inches. Diameter: 14 inches. Boardman & Co., c. 1825–35. (Courtesy of the Henry Francis du Pont Winterthur Museum)

Set of five measures, half gallon to gill. Heights: 9¹⁄₁₆, 6¾, 5¹⁄₁₆, 3¾, and 3 inches. Boardman and Hart, 1828–53. Extreme right: half gill measure. Height: 2 inches. T. D. Boardman, 1804–60. (Courtesy of the Brooklyn Museum)

Late porringer. Diameter: 4½ inches. Depth: 1⁹⁄₁₆ inches. Flagg & Homan, Cincinnati, 1842–54. (Private collection)

Inkwell. Boardman and Hart, 1828–53. (Private collection)

Soap box with hinged cover. Ashbil Griswold, 1807–35. (The Metropolitan Museum of Art. Gift of Mrs. Stephen S. Fitz-Gerald, 1962)

Inkwell. Boardman & Hall, 1844–45. (The Metropolitan Museum of Art. Gift of Mrs. J. Insley Blair, 1941, in memory of J. Insley Blair)

Coaster with band of decorative engraving. Oliver Trask, 1832–39. (The Metropolitan Museum of Art. Gift of Mrs. J. Insley Blair, 1941, in memory of J. Insley Blair)

Toy pigeon-breasted teapot. Height: 4½ inches. Attributed to Roswell Gleason. (Private collection.

Toy mug. Height: 2 inches. Diameter at top: 1¹⁵⁄₁₆ inches. Unmarked. (Private collection)

Ladle. James Weekes, 1822–35. (The Metropolitan Museum of Art. Gift of Mrs. J. Insley Blair, 1941, in memory of J. Insley Blair)

Ladle. Length: 14 inches. Wood handle. Lewis Kruiger, 1833. (Private collection)

Screw-top tankard, or priest's cann. Height: 4⅝ inches. Roswell Gleason, 1821–71. (The Metropolitan Museum of Art. Gift of Mrs. J. Insley Blair, 1940, in memory of J. Insley Blair.)

Spitoon. Height: 3 3/16 inches. Josiah Danforth, 1830–c. 1843. (Courtesy of the Henry Francis du Pont Winterthur Museum as shown in "Brittania in America" by Nancy Goyne, Winterthur Portfolio II)

Set of five spoons. Length: 5⅝ inches. J. G. Baldwin, c. 1840. (Private collection)

Demijohn. J. Putnam, 1830–55. (The Metropolitan Museum of Art. Gift of Mrs. J. Insley Blair, 1941, in memory of J. Insley Blair)

Biographies of Prominent Pewterers

A brief biography of those workers of greatest interest to collectors is given below. The dates next to the names are the working dates.

The Beverly, Massachusetts, Group: Philip Lee (ca. 1807–12), __?__ **Creesy** (ca. 1807–12), **Israel Trask** (ca. 1813–56), **Oliver Trask** (1832–39), and **Eben Smith** (1814–56)

Recent research by Nancy Goyne Evans of Winterthur has placed the beginning of the brittania industry in Massachusetts in the first decade of the nineteenth century. Philip Lee was born in 1786 on the Isle of Jersey and came to America before he was twenty-one. He started a brittania business in Beverly with a man named Creesy which was known as Lee and Creesy from 1807 to 1812. They sold out to Israel Trask, a silversmith, in 1812. Trask employed his brothers, George and Oliver, Oliver later going into business for himself. Eben Smith, a cabinet maker, made handles for Trask and then also went into business for himself around 1814. The shortage of brittania teapots imported from England due to the War of 1812 was exploited by Trask, who quickly became successful selling his teapots and creamers to Boston shops. The early pots of Lee and of Trask were in the Federal style, oval cylinders made of sheet metal and seamed lengthwise. The Trasks and Smith used this method for other items as well. All the members of this group worked in similar manners and styles using the distinctive decorative engraving of the silversmith. Israel Trask and Eben Smith continued in business until about 1856, making a variety of wares and using new techniques as the times demanded.

The Boardmans: Thomas Danforth Boardman (1804–60 and after), Sherman Boardman (1810–50), Timothy Boardman (1822–25)

Thomas Danforth Boardman was born in Litchfield, Connecticut, in 1784 and his brother Sherman in 1787. The family moved to Hartford, where Thomas D. began his career in 1804 with his brother joining him later. In 1822, the prospering Boardmans sent their younger brother, Timothy, to New York to take charge of their new branch. Only two years later Timothy died and the "T.B. & Co." mark was changed to "Boardman & Co." When the new manager, Lucius Hart, became a partner in 1827 the business became "Boardman & Hart." In 1844, a second branch was opened in Philadelphia under the name of "Boardman & Hall," with Sherman's son, Henry S. Boardman, and F. D. Hall in charge. The name was later changed to Hall, Boardman and Company and then to Hall and Boardman. Thomas D. Boardman discovered a formula for brittania metal in 1806 and kept it secret until 1821 when he divulged it to his young cousin, Josiah Danforth, in order to help him in his beginning business. A journeyman in Josiah's employ soon spread the secret.

The largest single American pewter business was that of the Boardmans of Hartford. Their existing pewter outnumbers in quantity and variety that of any other shop. Almost every nineteenth-century form made in pewter was made by them. With aggressive merchandising methods, their wares were sold throughout the East.

William Calder (1817–56)

As a boy Calder worked for Samuel E. Hamlin and about 1817 opened his own shop in Providence, Rhode Island. His work begins in the first period with the purchase of molds for eight- and nine-inch plates, mugs, and porringers. As the demand changed, Calder produced a wide range of brittania items to meet it.

94

Rufus Dunham (1837–60)

After working as a journeyman for Allen Porter and then Roswell Gleason, Dunham went into business for himself in 1837 in Westbrook, Maine. He moved to Portland in 1851 after a fire which burned his buildings. After that, his sons Joseph and Frederick became partners and the name was changed to Rufus Dunham & Sons, under which name it continued until 1882.

Roswell Gleason (1822–71)

Gleason was born in Putney, Vermont, in 1799. He moved to Dorchester, Massachusetts, in 1818 and opened his own shop for the making of block-tin and pewter in 1822 and started using brittania about 1830. In 1837 he received an award from the Massachusetts Charitable Mechanic Association for the high quality of his products. His business grew until at one point he employed one hundred and twenty men. He continued in business until 1871 although after 1850 many of his products were plated ware. Along with the Boardmans of Hartford and Reed and Barton at Taunton, Gleason was one of the three largest producers of brittania.

Ashbil Griswold (1807–35)

Griswold was apprenticed to Thomas Danforth III in Stepney, Connecticut, and in 1807 moved to the outskirts of Meriden to start his own business. Here he made basins, plates, dippers, porringers, tea and coffee pots, sugar bowls, and soap boxes, expanding to twelve employees by 1830, and going on to become the largest supplier of brittania in Connecticut after the Boardmans. His business ended with the formation of the Meriden Brittania Company in 1852.

A group of items made by Ashbil Griswold which show him to be a transitional pewterer between the first and second periods.

Allen Porter (1830–38) and **Freeman Porter** (1835–60 and later)

Allen Porter began making pewter in Westbrook, Maine, about 1830. In 1835, he was joined by his brother, Freeman, in a partnership, A. and F. Porter. Apparently, Allen left the business about 1839 while Freeman continued until the Civil War making lamps, candlesticks, teapots, and water pitchers.

George Richardson (1818–45)

Richardson was born in England around 1782. He was a pewterer in Boston from 1818 to 1828 and some time before 1840 moved to Cranston, Rhode Island, where he continued as a pewterer until his death in 1848. He is a transitional worker who made wares in the old manner and then became an early user of brittania.

Sellew & Co. (1832–60)

Enos and Osman Sellew migrated to Cincinnati, Ohio, from Philadelphia after having learned the craft in Connecticut. They formed the firm of Sellew & Co. in 1832 and about 1836 another brother, William, joined them. The firm's high quality of workmanship was recognized by the award of a certificate of merit by the Ohio Mechanics Institute in 1839. They went out of business about 1860.

Eben Smith

See Beverly Group.

The Taunton, Massachusetts, group of successor companies: Babbitt and Crossman (1823–27), **Babbitt, Crossman & Co.** (1827–29), **Crossman, West & Leonard** (1829–30), **Taunton Brittania Manufacturing Co.** (1830–37), **Leonard, Reed & Barton** (1837–40), **Reed & Barton** (1840 to present)

This group of companies made many of the typical brittania products, especially lamps, candlesticks, flagons and communion services, tea and coffee pots, and became one of the largest producers of brittania ware.

Israel Trask

See Beverly Group.

Oliver Trask

See Beverly Group.

5

Lamps

The American whale oil lamp is the most truly American form of pewter despite the fact that it is based upon a patent by the Englishman John Miles. Since the American lamps bear little resemblance to those made elsewhere, a collector can quickly learn to recognize them. Such an astonishing variety exists that this category alone would provide the basis for an extensive collection.

From the earliest times until the late eighteenth century, no substantial progress had been made in lamp design. Hollowed-out stones were used in prehistoric times to burn grease. When olive oil became abundant around the Mediterranean, float lamps, which are open lamps with the wick floated on the surface of the oil, were used. Their antiquity is proved by a handsome example of alabaster found in Tut-Ankh-Amen's tomb. Spout lamps, another variation of the oil lamp in which the wick is enclosed in a tube or spout, were used to burn oil in the Near East. Central Europe, lacking oil, resorted to animal fats which were burned in various types of open pan lamps, whose best known descendant is the betty lamp. This, together with various wood and rush-burning devices, and of course, candles, constituted the means of lighting well into the fourth quarter of the eighteenth century.

Then, in 1787, a quantum jump was made when John Miles of Birmingham, England, patented his agitable lamp which claimed "to give Perfect Light though ever so much Agitated." Its outstanding feature was the first enclosed nonspillable reservoir for oil with the wick and wick-tube supported vertically above the oil pool. Once having been invented, it seems astonishing that no one had thought of it before. This spill-proof font, when combined with the whale-oil burner, became our whale-oil lamp. Made of glass, tin, brass, and pewter, it came to be widely used in this country.

The Miles lamp was not long in coming to America as shown by an advertisement in the *Columbian Sentinal* of Boston for February 8, 1800. It reads:

Agitable Lamps

which are so constructed as to prevent the oil from spilling although the lamp should be overturned or thrown in any direction, made after the much approved ones called "Miles" Patent Lamps; and warranted to be equal to them in every particular, by Joseph Howe, near the Boston Stone, and for Sale, Wholesale and Retail, either plain, polished or japanned and of any form.

   N.B. all kinds of Tin Ware, plain and polished as usual.

Another advertisement in *J. Russell's Gazette* for February 24, 1800, reads:

Spermaceti-Oil for burning in Lamps. Best strained Sperm Oil by the hhd. bbl. or small quantity for sale . . . also Patent Lamps and Wicking . . . N.B. The Lamps are so constructed as not to spill when overset.

This establishes that whale oil as lamp fuel was available for the Miles Lamp in Boston by 1800.

Miles also described the whale-oil burner in his patent, although it is only incidental to his basic idea, the enclosed reservoir. Such burners have one or more cylindrical wick tubes, usually slightly tapered, which are set into a horizontal burner plate. The wick tubes extend well below the burner plate in order to provide some preheating of the thick oil, but only a short distance above it. They have vertical slots through which picks can be inserted to adjust the wick. In order to keep the air pressure constant in the reservoir as the oil is heated, a small opening is made in the burner plate. This may also serve to admit drips back into the font. The earliest whale-oil burners were held by cork disks, but after 1830 the burner was threaded to screw into a metal collar.

The use of more than one wick tube is often attributed to Benjamin Franklin, who is known to have observed that the light given by two candles, when the flames warm each other, is greater than the total light given by two individual candles. Professor Edwin B. Rollins has tested whale-oil lamps with one, two, and three wick burners to determine their candle power. He found that, on average, a two-tube burner produced 2.25 times as much light as a one-tube burner, while a three-tube burner produced 3.86 times as much as a single. Two-burner pewter whale-oil lamps are common but three-burner ones extremely rare.

Although whale-oil lamps were in use early in the nineteenth century, the great outburst of pewter lamp production occurred after 1825. New

Lamp burners. Left: whale oil burners. Overall height: 1½ inches. Diameter of burner plate: 1 inch. Right: Pair of splayed-out camphene burners with caps.

and cheaper methods of pewter manufacture by spinning and stamping, coupled with the increased availability of whale oil, brought this about. The main period of pewter whale-oil lamp output coincides and is associated with the adventurous and romantic American whaling industry.

The American whale fishery was one of the greatest maritime adventures in history. The *Mayflower* charter granted its company "all royal fishes, whales, balan, sturgeons and other fishes." The first colonial fishermen, aided by the local Indians, rowed about inshore waters in open boats in pursuit of the black right whales which migrated down along the coast. This evolved into an oceangoing whaling fleet which numbered three hundred and sixty by 1774. The hostilities of the Revolution decimated the fleet, leaving the industry prostrate at the end of the war.

When shipbuilding began again, it was concentrated on larger vessels fitted out for voyages of one, two, or three years in order to pursue the great sperm whale. The sperm whale yields more oil than other whales of comparable bulk and the oil from its blubber is of a finer quality than any other species, burning more brightly and with less smoke and odor. The most outstanding characteristic of this species is its huge square head. A light viscous wax called spermaceti, much prized for candles, was also obtained from this animal. Unlike the other large whales, it is a tropical- and warm-water creature, but its manifest superiority led the Americans on long voyages around the Cape of Good Hope as early as 1791.

Again the momentum of the whale fishery was interrupted by the embargo of 1807 and the War of 1812. By 1818 there were fewer than forty whalers left, but the New Englanders set to work rebuilding immediately upon cessation of hostilities. The economic structure of the union had also changed, for the industrial age had begun. Prior to the discovery of petroleum, animal and vegetable oils were of enormous importance to fill the vast needs for oils for heating, lighting, cooking, lubrication, and industrial uses. Whale oil was the most valuable and important such substance. This great demand spurred the rapid buildup which attained 203 vessels in 1829 and 421 in 1835. From about 1835 until the Civil War is popularly called the "golden age" of American whaling. Operations extended throughout the world and the industry was virtually an American monopoly. The high point was reached in 1846 when the fleet consisted of 736 vessels, employing more than seventy thousand men. After 1846, there was a slow decline hastened by a business recession in 1857. By 1853 gas made from coal was used for domestic and street lighting in the major cities. The industry's doom was sealed by the discovery of petroleum in 1859 and the *coup de grâce* administered by the outbreak of the Civil War.

Even while oil was pouring into the country from the whalers, a search was underway for a cheaper and better illuminant. Sperm oil became increasingly expensive and sold as high as $2.50 a gallon in 1840—about three times the price of regular whale oil. During the period from 1840 to 1860 lard oil cost from $1.00 to $2.50 a gallon. These were prohibitive costs for the average wage earner, who made less than $10.00 a week. Numerous burning fluids were developed among which was Porter's Burning Fluid, a combination of alcohol and turpentine, patented in 1835. The patent describes a means of removing water from alcohol and turpentine, since even a small amount of water causes the alcohol and turpentine to separate. Its brilliant white light and absence of smoke quickly brought it into widespread use. Many people tried it in their whale-oil lamps, sometimes with disastrous results. The fluid was highly inflammable and when overheated erupted out of the reservoir or exploded, causing many fires. Eventually, a new type of burner was developed called the camphene burner after camphene, a derivative of turpentine. These burners differ from the whale-oil ones in that the wick tubes are much longer above the burner plate, keeping the flame away from the reservoir and, in order to prevent preheating of the fluid, do not extend below it into the reservoir. They are generally made of brass, do not have slots, and splay out from one another when there is more than one. Small wick caps are usually provided to minimize evaporation of the volatile fluid when not in use as well as for extinguishing the flame. Some of the older whale-oil lamps were updated with the new burners, so that the age of a lamp does not always correspond with its burner. Early cast pewter lamps have been found with rather late camphene burners. With the camphene burner the final phase of the pewter lamp was reached. Kerosene burners came into use after 1860 and these were not made of pewter.

Standing Lamps

The most common style of pewter whale-oil lamp is the standing lamp, which consists of a whale-oil burner which screws into a variously shaped font or reservoir supported by a stem set on a wide flat base reminiscent of a candlestick. Most of the fonts have forms which are described as lozenge, acorn, lemon, cylinder, urn, or truncated cone. The most common of these is the simple cylinder. Forms are also combined, such as a cylinder with a lozenge bottom. A few like the hexagonal one by the Taunton Brittania Manufacturing Company fall outside this classification. The bases vary from dome-shaped to saucer and the stems vary in shape and height as well. Handles of various shapes occur on the font, stem, or base, although more generally there is no handle. Thus the permutations and combinations of font, stem, base, and handle are very nearly endless.

STYLES OF LAMPS

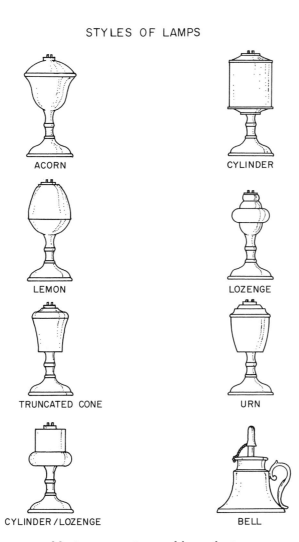

ACORN   CYLINDER

LEMON   LOZENGE

TRUNCATED CONE   URN

CYLINDER/LOZENGE   BELL

Most common types of lamp fonts

101

Whale oil lamp with cylindrical font. Overall height: 7¹³⁄₁₆ inches. R. Dunham, 1837–61. (Courtesy of the Henry Francis du Pont Winterthur Museum as shown in "Brittania in America" by Nancy Goyne, Winterthur Portfolio II)

Candlestick. Height: 6 inches. Same stem as whale-oil lamp on left. R. Dunham, 1831–61. (Private collection)

Whale oil lamp with lozenge font. Overall height: 8⅞ inches. Oliver Trask, 1832–39. (Courtesy of the Henry Francis du Pont Winterthur Museum as shown in "Brittania in America" by Nancy Goyne, Winterthur Portfolio II)

Whale oil lamp with acorn shape font, saucer base, and side handle on stem. Overall height: 7¼ inches. Brook Farm, 1844–47. (Courtesy of the Henry Francis du Pont Winterthur Museum as shown in "Brittania in America" by Nancy Goyne, Winterthur Portfolio II)

Pair of saucer base whale oil lamps, acorn shape fonts, saucer base, side handle on stem. Height: 7⅜ inches exclusive of burner. Reed & Barton, c. 1840–50. (Private collection)

Whale oil lamp with lemon shape font. Overall height: 8¼ inches. William Calder, c. 1841–56. (Courtesy of the Henry Francis du Pont Winterthur Museum, as shown in "Brittania in America" by Nancy Goyne, Winterthur Portfolio II)

Lamp with camphene burners, acorn shape font. Height: over-all, 10 inches. Allen Porter, 1830–38. (The Metropolitan Museum of Art. Gift of Mrs. J. Insley Blair, 1941, in memory of J. Insley Blair)

103

Whale oil lamp with lozenge font.
Height exclusive of burner: 6⅜ inches.
Unmarked. (Private collection)

Whale oil lamp with lozenge shape font.
Height exclusive of burner: 5½ inches.
Roswell Gleason, c. 1830–50. (Private collection)

Whale oil lamp, saucer base with ring handle,
lozenge-shape font. Height: 4½ inches. Roswell
Gleason, c. 1830–50. (Private collection)

Whale oil lamp, saucer base with ring handle,
acorn font. Height exclusive of burners: 5½ inches.
Morey and Ober, 1852–55. (Private collection)

Pair of saucer base whale oil lamps with truncated cone fonts. Height exclusive of burner: 5 inches. Unmarked. (Private collection)

Saucer base whale oil lamp with urn font. Height exclusive of burners: 4⅝ inches. Unmarked. (Private collection)

Small whale oil lamp of rare form. Height exclusive of burners: 4½ inches. Unmarked. (Private collection)

One of a pair of saucer base, whale oil lamps with urn font. Unmarked.

Double gimbel ship's lamp. Unmarked. Attributed to Endicott and Sumner, 1846–51. (Private collection)

Swinging, Swivel, or Gimbal Lamps

An addition to the household standing lamp is the swivel lamp, which can stand on a table or be hung on the wall with the base serving as a sconce. Such lamps are low, generally with a saucer base. The font swings from an arm fixed to the base so that the burner is vertical when the base is either horizontal or vertical. A further development of this principle appears in the double gimbal or ship's lamp in which the wick stays vertical with the pitching and rolling of the vessel. In this case the font is supported by a ring in which it swings which is in turn supported by an arm in which the ring swings. This ingenious lamp appears both marked and unmarked and is rather rare. Marked ones were made by Yale and Curtis and by Endicott and Sumner.

Sparking, Nursing, Courting, or Tavern Lamps

The most usual characteristic of this type of lamp, for which all of the above terms are used, is its small size, some being so small as to be classified as miniature at only one and a half inches tall. Since its purpose is to supply a "spark" of light, it generally has a single wick tube, which is smaller than that of the standard household lamp and consequently burns with a smaller flame. It was used wherever a dim light sufficed, such as a night light in the nursery or sick room, and as such was called a nursing lamp. Folklore has it that such a small lamp was set in the parlor when a young man came courting and signaled him that it was time to leave when the fuel was consumed. Probably the overwhelming use to which these lamps were put was to assist in retiring for the night. Their employment by taverns in this respect has earned them the name of tavern lamps. Hence it would appear that their small size was dictated by frugality rather than romance.

Pair of unmarked lamps with camphene burners. Left: Combination lozenge and cylinder font. Overall height: 8 inches. Right: Bell shape with side handle. Height exclusive of burner: 2⅜ inches. (Private collection)

Elongated beehive form camphene lamp. Height exclusive of burners: 3¹⁄₁₆ inches. Base diameter: 4¹⁄₁₆ inches. Capen & Molineux, N. Y., 1848–54. (Private collection)

Footed cylindrical font camphene lamp with side handle. Height exclusive of burners: 3⅛ inches. Capen & Molineux; N. Y., 1848–54. (Private collection)

Footed cylindrical camphene lamp with side handle. Height exclusive of burners: 2⅝ inches. William McQuilken, Philadelphia, 1845–53. (Private collection)

Small chamber whale oil lamp. Overall height: 2³⁄₁₆ inches. Taunton Brittania Manufacturing Co., 1830–36. (Courtesy of the Henry Francis du Pont Winterthur Museum as shown in "Brittania in America" by Nancy Goyne, Winterthur Portfolio II)

Pair of small chamber whale oil lamps. Height: 2¾ inches. Unmarked. (Private collection)

Group of lamps; from left to right: (a) Single bull's-eye lamp. Height: 8⅜ inches. Roswell Gleason; c. 1830-50; (b) Nursing, sparking, or chamber lamp. Height: 3½ inches. Capen & Molineux, 1848-54; (c) Standing lamp with camphene burners. Height: 11 inches. Capen & Molineux, 1848-54; (d) Double-arm patent lamp. Height: 8½ inches. Yale & Curtis, 1858-67; (e) Swinging lamp. Height: 5½ inches. Endicott & Sumner, 1846-51; (f) Standing lamp with saucer base. Height: 12 inches. Henry Hopper, 1842-47. (Courtesy of the Booklyn Museum)

Bullseye Lamps

The bullseye lamp was made by Roswell Gleason of Dorchester, Massachusetts. Such lamps, which are quite rare, consist of the addition of one, two, or more convex or magnifying lenses fixed next to the flame. The lenses serve to concentrate the light in a particular area much like a searchlight or slide projector. A secondary benefit was wind shielding, which lessened the effect of flickering. A prototype for such lamps is the student's, monk's, or lacemaker's lamp of medieval times in which open globes filled with water were used to focus the candle light for close work.

Lard-oil Lamps

Lard-oil lamps differ from whale-oil lamps only in the burner, which used a wide, flat wick in order to accommodate the thick lard oil. Lard oil from "prairie whales" or hogs was used extensively between 1840 and 1860 because it was readily available. It was a heavy, yellowish fluid which was a byproduct of lard-making. The best grade lard oil remained liquid at fairly low temperatures, but the common grades of the oil had to be heated before they could be easily burned. Whale-oil burners had extensions into the reservoir, which provide such preheating. The scarcity of true lard-oil burners suggests that most people used the more common whale-oil burners with this fuel.

Peg or Socket and Petticoat Lamps

The term "peg" is an Americanism which denotes a lamp that was designed to be inserted into the sockets of candlesticks. The petticoat lamp is a peg lamp with a skirt added which could stand on a table as well. These are comparatively rare in pewter.

Lamp Makers

At first the pewter whale-oil lamps were cast in molds. Later these were spun on lathes on wooden forms as were the other pewter pieces of this period. The lathe-turning method was conducive to variety and it is in these pieces that the collector finds a wide range to choose from.

The vast majority of these lamps are found unmarked, probably because they were not sold on the premises by the maker but to wholesalers who sold them to various retail outlets. Mr. W. A. Macfarlane, an avid collector, estimates that in his experience one out of five lamps is marked. The marks are typical of this period, stamped or incised in the base. Occasionally a number occurs here also and this is presumed to be a mold or pattern number. Some of the makers who put out a variety of forms included lamps. Outstanding among these are the craftsman Roswell Gleason of Dorchester, Massachusetts (1822–71), William Calder of Providence, Rhode Island (1817–56), Israel Trask of Beverly, Massachusetts (1807–56), and Eben Smith (1813–56), also of Beverly, Massachusetts. The demand for lamps spawned a substantial number of specialists who made nothing but lamps. Capen and Molineux (1848–53) was the leading lamp maker in New York City. Some makers made only candlesticks in addition to lamps. Endicott and Sumner are noted for producing ship's lamps. Yale and Curtis, Thomas Wildes, Brook Farm, and Taunton Brittania made mostly lamps. Brook Farm is especially interesting since it was an experimental commune in West Roxbury, Massachusetts (1841–47), where Ephraim Capen worked as a pewterer. This venture was not a commercial success, so Mr. Capen went to New York City to form a partnership with George Molineux.

Pewterers Known to Have Made Lamps, with Their Working Dates

"L" indicates as known to have made lamps only.
"LC" indicates as known to have made lamps and candlesticks only.

Adams, Henry W.	New York City	1857	L
Archer, Ellis S.	Philadelphia	1842–50	L
Archer and Janney	St. Louis, Mo.	1847	L
Bailey and Putnam	Malden, Mass.	1830–35	
Boardman, Thomas Danforth	Hartford, Conn.	1804–60	
Boardman & Hall	Philadelphia, Pa.	1844–45	
Boardman & Hart	New York, N. Y.	1828–53	
Brook Farm	West Roxbury, Mass.	1844–47	
Buckley, Townsend M.	Troy, N. Y.	1854–57	L
Calder, William	Providence, R. I.	1817–56	
Capen and Molineux	New York City	1848–54	L
Capen, Ephraim	West Roxbury, Mass.	1844–47	L
Coburn, H. R.	Location unknown	ca. 1840	L
Dunham, Rufus	Westbrook, Maine	1837–60	
Endicott and Sumner	New York City	1846–51	LC
Flagg and Homan	Cincinnati, Ohio	1842–54	
Francis, Daniel	Buffalo, N. Y.	1833–42	L
Fuller and Smith	New London, Conn.	ca. 1850–54	LC
Gleason, Roswell	Dorchester, Mass.	1821–71	
Graves, Henry H.	Middletown, Conn.	1849–51	
Hall, Almer	Wallingford, Conn.	1827–60	
Holmes, Robert & Sons	Baltimore, Md.	1853–54	
Hopper, Henry	New York City	1842–47	

Horsford, E. N.	Location unknown	1830's	L
Houghton and Wallace	Philadelphia	1843	L
Hyde, Martin	New York City	1857–58	L(
Jones, Edward	New York City	1837–50	L
Lawrence, William	Meriden, Conn.	1831–34	L
Leonard, Reed, & Barton	Taunton, Mass.	1835–45	
Marston, _____	Baltimore, Md.	1840's	
Meriden Britannia Co.	Meriden, Conn.	1852 on	
Morey and Ober	Boston, Mass.	1852–55	
Morey, Ober and Co.	Boston, Mass.	1855–57	
Morey and Smith	Boston, Mass.	1857–60 on	
Neal, I.	Location unknown	1842	L
Newell, Caldwell & Coffin	Boston, Mass.	1853	
Ostrander and Norris	New York City	1848–50	L(
Parker, J. G.	Rochester, N. Y.	1840 on	
Parmenter, W. H.	Location unknown	1840's	L
Porter, Allen	Westbrook, Maine	1830–38	
Porter, Freeman	Westbrook, Maine	1835–60 on	
Putnam, James H.	Malden, Mass.	1830–55	
Reed and Barton	Taunton, Mass.	1840 on	
Renton and Co.	New York City	1830's	L
Rust, Samuel	New York City	1837–45	L
Sellew and Company	Cincinnati, Ohio	1832–60	
Sickel and Shaw	Philadelphia	1849–50	L
Smith, Eben	Beverly, Mass.	1814–56	
Smith & Co.	Boston, Mass.	1847–49	
Stalkamp, J. H. & Co.	Cincinnati, Ohio	1853–56	
Starr, William H.	New York City	1843–46	L
Taunton Britannia Mfg. Co.	Taunton, Mass.	1830–34	
Tomlinson, Harvey	Geneva, N. Y.	1843	
Trask, Israel	Beverly, Mass.	ca. 1813–56	
Vose and Co.	Albany, N. Y.	1840's	
Walker, _____	New York City	after 1840	
Weekes, James	Brooklyn and New York City	ca. 1820–33	
Weekes, J. & Co.	Poughkeepsie, N. Y.	1833–43	
Wildes (Wilds), Thomas	Philadelphia	1829–33	L(
	New York City	1833–40	L(
Woodbury, J. B.	Beverly, Mass.	1830–35	
	Philadelphia	1835–38	
Woodbury & Colton	Location unknown	1835–36	
Yale & Curtis	New York City	1858–67	L

6

Cleaning, Fakes, and Reproductions

Cleaning

Pewter grass, horsetails, and scouring grass are common names for the plant equisetum hiemale which was used by the early housewife to keep her pewter bright as well as for other scouring jobs in the kitchen. When used with soft soap or wood ash to add alkalinity, such grass is reputed to have been very effective in removing food as well as tarnish from the surface of pewter articles. Clean, gleaming pewter was a point of pride in the well-run household.

Today, however, there is no such unanimity of opinion about the finish on displayed pewter. There are those who prefer it bright and new-looking as did the early housewife, while at the other extreme there are those who like it dull and even crusty, exhibiting the full patina of the ages. A majority of English collectors keep their collections bright and clean on the large surfaces, leaving patina in the details of corners, moldings, designs, and surface irregularities. Another group prefers a light gray tone, which is livened by waxing. This is a matter of individual choice that only the collector himself can make.

To some extent the choice is narrowed by the condition of the piece. If the tarnish is thin with a metallic gleam underneath and if there are no pits or thick crusts of corrosion, the collector has several options open to him. If, on the other hand, the piece has a thick, brittle crust or areas which are heavily pitted, the decision on the steps to be taken should be made by someone with experience and not rashly attempted by the amateur. Indiscriminate cleaning of a badly encrusted piece could reveal holes where the corrosion has eaten right through the metal, or a heavily pock-marked surface which requires extensive filling or mechanical buffing to look presentable. This should serve as a warning to the purchaser that a heavy layer of corrosion masks the true condition of pewter. Most pewter dealers clean their pewter so that the surface is revealed. Do not underestimate the magnitude of the task or the risk!

Pewter or brittania metal is largely tin which in ordinary household environments stays bright and polished for years. Slowly, however, oxides and other corrosion compounds form on the surface as a result of exposure to oxygen and other gases in the atmosphere. The surface dulls, then darkens, and for some alloys a crust develops. Somewhat mysteriously, some alloys develop pits where the pewter is eaten out.

One theory for the cause of this pitting is the nonhomogeneity of the metal. Spots exist where there are impurities, islands of foreign metals. Two dissimilar metals have an electrochemical potential between them, creating the effect of a battery. Normally, any current which flows goes through the metal separating the islands and no harm is done, but as corrosion builds on the surface another path for this current could develop. If this corrosion film is moistened by a humid atmosphere, the film becomes a conducting electrolyte and galvanic corrosion can occur on the surface of the pewter. As this process continues the corrosion eats deeply into the metal, causing a pit as the pewter and small metallic islands are eaten away. Although there is no remedy for the crudeness of eighteenth- and nineteenth-century refining techniques, the pitting can be controlled by keeping the pewter clean and in a dry atmosphere.

The tarnish coating is made up largely of the oxides of tin and the other metals in the alloy. If the coating is thin it can be washed off using Ajax brand liquid household detergent or some similar product applied with a pad of #0000 steel wool. If the layer is too thick for this method, one must resort to an abrasive or chemical cleaning. A good abrasive is finely ground pumice stone available at most hardware stores. It may be applied with either a pad of #0000 steel wool or a cloth which is first dipped in water and then in the pumice. After rubbing hard and long, the extremely tough surface tarnish will be removed but the patina will remain in the corners, joints, crevices, and surface irregularities. For a higher shine, the surface can be polished by rubbing lightly with a clean dry pad of #0000 steel wool. Although this mechanical abrasion technique for removing tarnish requires considerable effort, it is especially rewarding for articles which are only lightly corroded. Most collectors prefer the result to that obtained with a complete chemical cleaning.

Chemical cleaning involves dissolving the surface oxides in a solution which does not attack the pewter base. Oxides of tin are soluble in water providing the solution is either very acid (low pH) or very alkaline (high pH). Hydrochloric acid is often used for acid baths but is not recommended for home use. A practical and effective alkaline bath for the amateur can be made using common lye (sodium hydroxide), which is available at the supermarket. A lye solution will loosen or dissolve the tarnish without attacking the pewter.

Unless protection is provided, the chemical treatment will remove tarnish from the touch marks, crevices in and around moldings, and pits in the surface. A lye solution can harm the finish on wooden handles and finial buttons. If the wooden handles are not removable, they and special areas such as the touchmark can be protected with a coating of paraffin or vaseline. Unless small holes in hollow parts such as under handles are plugged, the piece may continue to drip lye, perhaps damaging some polished furniture surface as it slowly dries out, sometimes over a period of months.

Common-sense precautions should be taken when using the lye-cleaning bath. It is best done in an area such as a basement where the floor will not be damaged by drips; rubber gloves and old clothes should be worn, and children and pets barred from the area. A large plastic pail (garbage-pail size) makes a suitable container. Although it is not critical, about an ounce of lye to a gallon of water makes a satisfactory concentration. (Do not use the lye with aluminum chips made for cleaning kitchen drains.) The action is speeded by using hot water, but of course this is incompatible with the use of wax or vaseline.

Place the piece of pewter into the solution so that it is completely submerged. This is important, for an exposed area will leave an unsightly ring at the water line which is very difficult to remove. Keep the pewter in the solution from one-half hour to forty-eight hours, depending on the amount of corrosion. In order to judge when to remove it, make a test by taking it out of the bath (remember the rubber gloves) and rub a flat surface lightly with #000 or #0000 steel wool. If the tarnish does not come off with light rubbing, it is not ready and should be put back. Handles and spouts are made from a different alloy and are the last to relinquish their corrosion. Sometimes it will not succumb fully and it is necessary to rub briskly with steel wool or scrape an occasional area with a flat knife.

As soon as the piece is taken out of the lye solution, the tarnish should be removed with the aid of a brush or with a little light rubbing with the steel wool. Then the pewter must be thoroughly washed with clean water. Teapots and similar forms are best soaked in water for several hours. When dry, the surface of the metal has a smoky haze with patches of tarnish here and there. All of this is removed by rubbing with fine steel wool and pumice. After this procedure, the piece is washed in soap and water, dried, and shined with a clean dry piece of #0000 steel wool.

Once the metal has been restored to a clean condition, it can be kept that way by washing with very fine steel wool and Ajax Liquid Household Cleaner (or similar product). Under normal atmospheric conditions this does not need to be done more than once or twice a year.

Fakes

The lure of quick profit has led unscrupulous operators to take advantage of the collector in every field of art and antiques. One cannot be too sanguine after curators in the White House announced that a Baltimore secretary was a fake or after the admission of the Metropolitan Museum of Art in New York City concerning Etruscan statuary. Since the 1920's, English pewter has had its share of very well-made fakes, often from the original molds. Fortunately, American pewter has been largely free of such practices. The probability of getting a fake approaches zero if one buys from a competent and reputable dealer. Pieces where the family history is known are generally, but not always, safe. When assurances are given that an item has been in the family many, many years, these sincere avowals may apply to an object made in the 1920's, a period of great interest in Americana.

Rather than listing the specific fakes known to have been made, it is better to explain the categories of fakes and their methods of detection. Actually, only a few of any particular one are made, since the market clearly could not absorb a large number of specimens of a purported rarity. When the inevitable detection occurs, that particular forgery ceases and the forger must devise a new deception. Experience in handling authentic objects in addition to an understanding of the general principals will help the collector to avoid the most obvious pitfalls.

Problem pieces or fakes can be categorized as follows:

1. Reproductions not intended as fakes.
2. "Married" pieces, parts of different pieces joined to make one.
3. Deliberate addition of forged marks to a genuine old piece.
4. Total reproduction of a bogus piece including marks.

Modern reproductions which are made as decorative items for those who like and want pewter but can not afford or find the originals should pose no problem to the experienced collector. To anyone who has handled numerous pieces of old pewter, a reproduction does not "feel right." This "feel" is applicable to the detection of all classes of fakes. It is the mental integration of such factors as form, construction, weight, finish, overall patina, and the condition of the metal including pits, voids, and wear. Variations of patina are part of this "feel." A truly old and untouched item will have a different color and metal condition on the outside as against the inside, and on the top as opposed to the underside.

The construction of most recent reproduction is different from the eighteenth- and nineteenth-century models and those with imitation makers' marks often have obviously crude eagles cast or stamped into the metal. Reproduction plates are usually not skimmed and forms such as mugs are often cast in one mold, handle and all, with the mold mark clearly visible. A conscious attempt to understand the construction and aging process will aid in separating the reproduction from the genuinely old.

There is, however, one class of reproductions that is more difficult to detect. During the 1920's when pewter was in great demand, reproductions were made using the old techniques and copying the old forms. Not intended to deceive, these were made or sold by reputable businessmen such as Gebelein and W. I. Cowlishaw, both of Boston, and stamped with their names. Some reproductions by others are known to have gone out unmarked and after fifty years have developed some of the signs of age. Since metallurgy in the 1920's was far more advanced than a hundred years earlier, the metal in these reproductions is usually perfectly smooth without surface pits and voids.

Married pieces are made by the joining of parts from different old pieces and evidence of this should be sought. Fresh solder around the base of a pot or differences in finish or patina on the bottom as opposed to the sides of the interior are causes for concern. A poorly fitted top or one that is not consistent with the rest of the design requires further investigation. An obviously resoldered porringer handle or a porringer without its linen mark invites speculation. Was the original handle merely resoldered or were two parts scavenged to make a whole?

The detection of newly added marks to old unmarked pieces is made more difficult by the precision obtainable using modern photograph and metal working techniques. Such a piece will have all the signs of the genuine antique which it is. In order to detect the forgery, first check the form and maker. Is it an American form? The most likely source material for such forgeries are unmarked English items. Is the form consistent with the period in which the maker worked and is it a form known to have been made by him? After examining the form and construction, examine the mark closely. Sometimes it is helpful to check the mark against photographs as they appear in the books by Kerfoot or Laughlin. Small irregularities in the lettering and execution of the design that become a characteristic of the individual die can be observed in a photograph. Is the color of the metal different in the immediate area? Are small scratches obliterated or made discontinuous by the addition of the mark? Is the mark crisp or slurred? Are there any areas where a possible previous marking has been filed off? If any of these questions have unfavorable responses, the collector should hesitate until he has an expert opinion or more information.

If one comes up against a total counterfeit—the object itself plus the mark—detection will depend on how it was done. One way is to make castings from an original old object such as a plate. These will fail to be convincing because they lack the sharpness of detail of the original. Other than this, it is not possible to put into print safeguards which will protect one in every instance against the really superior cheat. The Pewter Collectors' Club of America publishes in its *Bulletin* detailed descriptions of suspicious pieces that come to the attention of its members. Such information is current and can be obtained from a member.

Actually, the problem of pewter fakes is not of great magnitude. The vast majority of that which is seen in the shops of reliable dealers and at antiques shows is genuine; so, there is no need to be frozen with fear and not enjoy collecting. The fruits of such a hobby are far greater than the small risk.

Collecting Old Reproductions

As far back as 1898, W. I. Cowlishaw of Boston made reproductions of the earlier shapes, using the traditional construction techniques of casting and spinning. These were marked by him with a small circular touch with the initials "W.I.C." and an eagle. He produced fine pieces for the next thirty years or so until the 1930's, when his business was continued by Morton Wheelock. Wheelock changed the eagle touch to a small shield touch with W. I. Cowlishaw, and worked until the 1940's. His output was mainly new forms for modern living such as a cake plate with porringer handles rather than reproductions of the older forms.

Reproduction lamps, c. 1927. (Courtesy of Gebelein Silversmiths)

Reproduction whale oil lamps, spun. Unmarked. Boston, 1928.

In the 1920's, Gebelein Silversmiths (and Pewterers) of Boston put out a catalog and advertised an extensive selection of both reproduction and modern pewter forms. Many of these pieces were made by Reed and Barton, and Grandmount, both of Taunton, Massachusetts. They were marked with the manufacturer's or the Gebelein name. Many of these pieces by Cowlishaw, Gebelein, and others are becoming venerable enough to be collectable themselves.

During the intervening years many others have produced pewter items for use in the modern household. Most of these have only casual association with the antique. Others, such as the offerings by the International Silver Company, reproduce dent-for-dent pieces in their own or other collections. The markings on these should preclude even the most naive of collectors from mistaking them for antique.

There are various reasons for collecting, some of which are a mystery to the noncollector. There is also much gratuitous advice on how and what to collect, but the best is for the collector to arm himself with as much information as possible.

American Pewterers and Their Marks

This list of pewterers includes only those with known surviving examples. Each listing includes the name of the pewterer or firm, approximate working dates, and place of business. The listing is numbered, and for each maker with more than one mark, the various marks and their components are labeled with the small letters of the alphabet: "a," "b," "c," etc. Thus a mark may be completely described by the assigned number plus the appropriate letters. In general, the line name marks of the later makers are not sketched. For those who wish to refer to a photograph of a mark, an "L" number is given which refers to the figure number of the photograph in *Pewter in America, Its Makers and Their Marks,* Volumes I, II, and III, by Ledlie I. Laughlin.

Pewterers with no known surviving examples are listed separately.

Adams, Henry W.   (1)
New York City, 1857

Allison, Andrew   (2)
Philadelphia, Pa., 1837–41

Archer and Janney   (3)
(Benjamin Archer and N. E. Janney)
St. Louis, Mo., 1847

Armitages and Standish   (4)
Location unknown, 1837 and later

Austin, Nathaniel   (5)
Charlestown, Mass., 1763–1807
  a. L 297

b. L 298

c. L 300

d. L 299

e. L 301

f. L 296, used
   on quart mugs

Austin, Richard (6)
Boston, Mass., 1793–1817

a. L 304   b. L 306

c. L 305   d. L 307

also used (9), c

Babbitt, Crossman and Co. (7)
(Isaac Babbitt, Wm. W. Crossman)
Taunton, Mass., 1828–29

a.

Babbitt and Crossman (8)
Taunton, Mass., 1824–27

Badger, Thomas (9)
Boston, Mass., 1787–1815

a. L 308   b. L 309

c. L 287

Bailey and Brainard (10)
Cobalt, Conn., after 1840

Bailey and Putnam (11)
Malden, Mass., 1830–35

a.   b.

Baker, John (12)
Boston, Mass., 1674–96
a. attributed, L 876

Baldwin, D. S. (13)
Conn., ca. 1840–50

Baldwin, Jesse G. (14)
Middletown, West Meriden, Conn., 1840–50

Ball, William (15)
Philadelphia, Pa., 1775–81

Barn(e)s, Blak(e)slee (16)
Philadelphia, Pa., 1812–17

a. L 551   b. L 556

c. L 557   d. L 553

f. L 554   e. L 555

g. L 558, incised

Barns, Stephen (17)
Conn., ca. 1791–1800

a. L 417

Bartholdt, William (18)
Williamsbugh, N. Y., 1850–54

Bassett, Francis I (19)
New York, N. Y., 1718–58
indistinguishable from marks of Francis II (20)

Bassett, Francis II (20)

New York City, 1754–80, 1785–99
Horsetown, Cranetown, N. J., 1780–85, marks may have been used by either (19) or (20), Francis, I or II

a. L 456

b. L 457

c. L 459

d. L 460

e. L 461

f. L 462

Bassett, Frederick (21)

New York City, 1761–80, 1785–99
Hartford, Conn., 1780–85

a. L 463

b. L 464

c. L 465

d. L 466

e. L 467   f. L 468

g. L 861

may have used (20), b

Bassett, John (22)

New York City, 1720–61

a. L 458   b. L 860

Belcher, Joseph (23)

Newport, R. I., 1769–76

a. L 313

may have used (22), b

Belcher, Joseph, Jr. (24)

Newport, R. I., 1776–84
New London, Conn., 1784–87

a. L 314

b. L 315

also used (23), a

Benham, Morris   (25)
West Meriden, Conn., 1849

Bidgood (see Plumly and Bidgood)   (26)

Billings, William   (27)
Providence, R. I., 1791–1806
   a. L 346   b. L 347

Boardman, Henry S.   (28)
Philadelphia, Pa., 1844–61
Hartford, Conn., 1841

   a. Incised   BOARDMAN

PHILADA

Boardman, Luther   (29)
South Reading, Mass., 1834–37
Meriden, Conn., 1837–39
   a.   b.   L.B.

Boardman, Luther & Co.   (30)
Chester, Conn., 1839–42
East Haddam, Conn., 1842–70

Boardman, Thomas D.   (31)
Hartford, Conn., 1804–after 1860
   a. used 1805–20, L 424

b. L 425

c. L 426   d. L 427

e. L 434, starting   f. L 433, ca. 1820–30
   ca. 1810

g. L 430, after 1820   h. L 435 1830 on
                              (81), h

Boardman, T. D. and S.   (32)
(Thomas D. and Sherman Boardman)
Hartford, Conn., 1810–30

   a. L 428   b. L 429

   TD&SB   TD&SB

Boardman, Timothy & Co.   (33)
(Timothy Boardman and Lucius Hart)
New York City, 1822–25

   a. L 432   TB&Cᵒ

Boardman & Co (34)
New York City, 1825–27

a. L 431
(31), g

Boardman and Hall (35)
(Henry S. Boardman and Franklin D. Hall)
Philadelphia, Pa., 1844–45

a.

Boardman and Hart (36)
(Thomas D. Boardman and Lucius Hart)
New York City, 1828–53

a. L 436 earliest N. Y. touch

b. L 437 and 438   c. L 437 and 439

Bonyge, Robert (37)
Boston, Mass., 1731–63, attributed marks

a. L 292   b. L 835

c. (9), c .

Boyd, Parks (38)
Philadelphia, Pa., 1795–1819

a. L 544   b. L 545

c. L 546

Boyle, Robert (39)
New York City, 1752–58

a. L 493   b. L 494

Bradford, Cornelius (40)
New York City, 1752–53, 1770–85
Philadelphia, Pa., 1753–70

a. L 495

b. L 496 and 497

125

Bradford, William, Jr. (41)
New York City, 1719–58, attributed marks
  a. L 581   b. L 583   c. L 584

Braman, Elijah, Warren, R. I., 1832–39 (42)

Bridgen, Timothy (43)
Albany, N. Y., 1804–19
  a. L 519

Brook Farm (44)
West Roxbury, Mass., 1844–47
  a.

Brower, A. (45)
New York City, ca. 1820

Brown, E. & Co. (46)
Location unknown, ca. 1820

Brunstrom, John Andrew (46)
Philadelphia, Pa., 1781–93
  a. L 870

  b. L 867

(179), c

Buckley, Townsend M. (47)
Troy, N. Y., 1854–57

Bull & Lyman (48)
Meriden, Conn., ca. 1845

Bull, Lyman & Couch (49)
(—— Bull, William Lyman, Ira Couch)
Meriden, Conn., 1845–49

Byles, Thomas (50)
Newport, R. I., 1711–12
Philadelphia, Pa., 1738–71
  a. L 586

(46), b, also used by
"Love" and John A. Brunstrom

Cahill, J. W. & Co. (51)
Location unknown, after 1830

Calder, William (52)
Providence, R. I., 1817–56
  a. L 350   b. L 351

Calverley, John (53)
Philadelphia, Pa., 1840–41

Campbell, Samuel (54)
Baltimore, Md., 1814–18
  a. L 453

Capen, Ephraim (55)
West Roxbury, Mass., 1844–47
New York City, 1847–54

Capen and Molineux (56)
(Ephraim Capen and George Molineux)
New York City, 1848–54

a.

b.

Carlstedt, J. N. (57)
Rockford, Ill., after 1840

Carnes, John (58)
Boston, Mass., 1723–60
a. L 285

Cincinnati Britannia Co. (59)
Cincinnati, Ohio, ca. 1850

Coburn, H. R (60)
Location unknown, ca. 1840

Coldwell, George (61)
New York City, 1787–1811

a. L 508

b. L 509 or 510

Colten, Oren (62)
Philadelphia, Pa., 1835–38

a. O.COLTON

Copeland, Joseph (63)
Chuckatuck, Jamestown, Va., 1675–91

a.

Cotton, —— (see Hall and Cotton) (64)
Middlefield, Conn., ca. 1840–45

Creesy, —— (see Lee and Creesy) (65)
Beverly, Mass., ca. 1807–12

Crossman, Ebenezer (66)
Hudson, N. Y., ca. 1790–1800

a. L 862

b. L 863

Crossman, West, and Leonard (67)
(William W. Crossman, William A. West, and
Zephaniah Leonard)
Taunton, Mass., 1829–30

Curtiss, Daniel (68)
Albany, N. Y., 1822–40

a. L 522   b. L 523

Curtiss, E. and L. (69)
(Edwin E. and Lemuel J. Curtiss)
Meriden, Conn., ca. 1838–40

Curtiss, Frederick (70)
Glastonbury, Conn., ca. 1850

Curtiss, I.   (71)

Location unknown, ca. 1820-30

  a. L 430a   b. L 452

Curtiss, Joseph, Jr.   (72)

Troy, N. Y., 1827-32
Albany, N. Y., 1832-58

Curtiss, Lemuel J.   (73)

Meriden, Conn., 1836-52

Curtiss and Curtiss

(see (69), E. & L. Curtiss)

Cutler, David   (74)

Boston, Mass., 1730-65

  a. L 286

  b. L 287, same as
    Thomas Badger (9), c

Danforth, Edward   (75)

Hartford, Conn., 1786-95

  a. L 389   b. L 387

  c. L 388

  d. L 390

Danforth, John   (76)

Norwich, Conn., 1773-93

  a. L 352   b. L 355

  c. L 353

  d. L 354   e. L 357

Danforth, Joseph   (77)

Middletown, Conn., 1780-88

  a. L 374   b. L 375

  c. L 376

  d. L 378

  e. L 377

(82), e, partnership
with Thomas II, 1780-82

128

Danforth, Joseph, Jr. (78)

Richmond, Va., 1807–12

a. L 380 + 379

b. L 381

Danforth, Josiah (79)

Middletown, Conn., 1821–ca. 1843

a. L 394

b. L 395

Danforth, Samuel (of Norwich) (80)

Norwich, Conn., 1793–1802

a. L 359, 359a

b. L 358

(76) a, Norwich scroll

Danforth, Samuel (of Hartford) (81)

Hartford, Conn., 1795–1816

a. L 396

b. L 400

c. L 398

d. L 401

e. L 403

f. L 399

g. L 397

h. L 404, used later by
   Thomas D. Boardman

Danforth, Thomas, II (82)

Middletown, Conn., 1755–82

a. L 364

b. L 363

c. L 362

d. L 361

e. L 365, partnership with
   son (77) 1780–82

Danforth, Thomas, III (83)

Stepney, Conn., 1777–1818

Philadelphia, Pa., 1807–13

a. L 368

b. L 369

c. L 367

d. L 370

e. L 373

f. L 366

g. L 371

h. L 372

i. L 849

Danforth, William (84)

Middletown, Conn., 1792–1820

a. L 393

b. L 392, 392a

Day, Benjamin (85)

Newport, R. I., 1744–57

Derby, Thomas S. (86)

Middletown, Conn., 1822–50

a. L 441

b. L 443

De Riemer, Cornelius B. & Co. (87)

Auburn, N. Y., 1833

Dickinson, Charles (88)

Newark, N. J., 1850–57

Dolbeare, Edmund (89)

Boston, Mass., ca. 1671–84, ca. 1692–1706

Salem, Mass., 1684–92

a. L 831

Dolbeare, John (90)

Boston, Mass., 1690–1740, attributed marks

a. L 832

Dolbeare, Joseph (91)

Boston, Mass., ca. 1690–1704, same as John Dolbeare, marks attributed (90), a

Dunham, E. (92)

Location unknown, after 1825

Dunham, Rufus (93)

Westbrook, Maine, 1837–60

a.

b. Incised

R.DUNHAM

Dunham, R & Sons (94)

Portland, Maine, 1861

a. Incised

Dunlap, J & Co. **(95)**
Philadelphia, Pa., ca. 1830

Dunn, Cary **(96)**
New York City, ca. 1770–90

Eadem, Semper **(97)**
Boston, Mass., ca. 1740–80

a. L 290   b. L 287

c. L 291   d. L 835

e. L 838, with "IS"   f. L 836, with "TS"

Edgell, Simon **(98)**
Philadelphia, Pa., 1713–42

a. L 526   b. L 527, 528   c. L 529

Eggleston, Jacob **(99)**
Middletown, Conn., ca. 1796–1807
Fayetteville, N. C., 1807–13

a. L 385   b. L 386

c. L 852   d. L 851, 1807–13

Eldridge, Eli **(100)**
Taunton, Mass., 1848–60

Ellicott, George **(101)**
Bucks County, Pa., 1779

Elsworth, William J. **(102)**
New York City, 1767–98

a. L 506   b. L 505   c. L 504

Endicott, Edmund **(103)**
New York City, 1846–53

Endicott and Sumner **(104)**
(Edmund Endicott and William F. Sumner)
New York, N. Y., 1846–51

a.

Farnam, D. L. **(105)**
Location unknown, after 1825

Fenn, G. and J. **(106)**
(Gaius and Jason Fenn)
New York City, 1831–43

Flagg and Homan **(107)**
(Asa F. Flagg and Henry Homan)
Cincinnati, Ohio, 1842–54

Forbes, E. G. **(108)**
Location unknown, after 1830

131

Francis, Daniel (109)
Buffalo, N. Y., 1833–42

Frink, Nathaniel (110)
Northampton, Mass.?, ca. 1750

    a. L 846

Fryers, John (111)
Newport, R. I., 1749–68, attributed marks

    a. L 883

Fuller and Smith (112)
(Aaron Chauncey Fuller)
Pequonock Bridge, New London, Conn., ca. 1850–54

—— and Gardner (113)
Location unknown, after 1830

Gerhardi & Co. (114)
Now known to be English

Gleason, Roswell (115)
Dorchester, Mass., 1821–71

    a.   b.   c.

    d. Incised ROSWELL GLEASON

Glennore Co. (116)
(see George Richardson)
Cranston, R. I., after 1825

Graham and Savage (117)
(Jasper Graham and W. H. Savage)
Middletown, Conn., 1837

Graves, Henry H. (118)
Middletown, Conn., 1849–51

    a.

GRAVES

Graves, Joshua B. (119)
Troy, N. Y., 1847–49
Middletown, Conn. 1849

Graves, J. B. & H. H. (120)
Middletown, Conn., 1852

Graves and Whitlock (121)
(Joshua B. Graves and John H. Whitlock)
Troy, N. Y., 1848–49

Green, Samuel (122)
Boston, Mass., 1779–1828

    a. L 302, 839   b. L 303

Griswold, Ashbil (123)
Meriden, Conn., 1807–35

    a. L 418, (1807–15)   b. L 419, (1807–20)

    c. L 420, ca. 1820–30   d. L 421, ca. 1820–30

    A·G

Griswold, Giles (124)
Augusta, Ga., 1818–20

    a. L 601, 601a   b. L 874

Griswold, Sylvester (125)
Baltimore, Md., 1820

a. L 570

Hall, Boardman & Co. (126)
(Franklin D. Hall and Henry S. Boardman)
Philadelphia, Pa., 1846–48

Hall, Elton and Co. (127)
(Almer Hall and William Elton)
Wallingford, Conn., 1847–60 and later

Hall and Boardman (128)
(Franklin D. Hall and Henry S. Boardman)
Philadelphia, Pa., 1849–57

Hall and Cotton (129)
(Nelson Hall and —— Cotton)
Middlefield, Conn., ca. 1840–45

Hamlin, Samuel (130)
Hartford, Middletown, Conn., 1767–73
Providence, R. I., 1773–1801
  Samuel, Sr. only:

a. L 843   b. L 844

c. L 332   d. L 334

Used by father and
son, Samuel E.:

e. L 330

f. L 331

g. L 333    h. L 336

Hamlin, Samuel E. (131)
Providence, R. I., 1801–56
  See (130), e,f,g,h,
  Samuel E. only:

a. L 337   b. L 338

c. L 335

Harbeson, —— (132)
Philadelphia, Pa., ca. 1800

a. L 549

Harrison, Joseph (133)
Philadelphia, Pa., 1829–52

Hart, Lucius D. (134)
New York, N. Y., 1828–ca. 1853

Hattersley and Dickinson (135)
(William Hattersley and Charles Dickinson)
Newark, N. J., 1854–56

H. D. and H. (136)
(Wm. Hattersley, Chas. Dickinson, J. Hattersley)
Newark, N. J., 1851–56

Hera, C. and J. (137)
Philadelphia, Pa., 1800–12

  a. L 543

Hersey, Samuel S. (138)
Belfast, Maine, ca. 1840–60

Heyne, Johann Christopher (139)
Bethlehem, Tulpehocken, Pa., 1742–56
Lancaster, Pa., ca. 1756–80

  a. L 530   b. L 532

  c. L 533

  d. L 589, possibly
    J. C. Horan

Hinsdale, J. and D. (140)
(John and Daniel Hinsdale)
Middletown, Conn., 1810–26

  a. L 446

Holmes, Robert & Sons (141)
Baltimore, Md., 1853–54

Holt, Thomas R. (142)
Meriden, Conn., 1845–49

Homan, Henry (143)
Cincinnati, Ohio, 1847–64

Homan and Co. (144)
(Henry Homan and Asa F. Flagg)
Cincinnati, Ohio, 1847–90

Hopper, Henry (145)
New York City, 1842–47

  a.

Horsford, E. N. (146)
Location unknown, after 1830

Houghton and Wallace (147)
Philadelphia, Pa., 1843

Humiston, Willis (148)
Troy, N. Y., 1841–52

Hunt, S. (149)
Location unknown, after 1830

Hyde, Martin (150)
New York City, 1857–58

Johnson, Jehiel (151)
Fayetteville, N. C., 1818–19
Middletown, Conn., 1815–25

  a. L 447   b. L 448   c. L 449, 449a

Jones, Edward (152)
New York City, 1837–50

Jones, Gershom (153)
Providence, R. I., 1774–1809

  a. L 339

  b. L 340

c. L 341

d. L 342

e. L 343

f. L 344

g. L 345

Kaufman, Earnest (154)
Philadelphia, Pa., 1855

Keene, Josiah (155)
Providence, R. I., 1801–17

a. L 348   b. L 349

Kilbourn, Samuel (156)
Baltimore, Md., 1814–39

a. L 568   b. L 569

Kimberly, DeWitt (157)
Meriden, Conn., 1845–49

Kirby, Peter (158)
New York City, 1736–88

a. L 498

Kirby, William (159)
New York City, 1760–93

a. L 499   b. L 502

c. L 500

d. L 501

e. L 503

Kirk, Elisha (160)
York, Pa., 1780–90

a. L 547

Knight, W. W. & Co. (161)
Philadelphia, Pa., 1840

Kruiger, Lewis (162)
Philadelphia, Pa., 1833

Lafetra, Moses (163)
New York City, 1812–16

a. L 511

Langworthy, Lawrence (164)
Newport, R. I., 1731–39

  a. L 311, used in
    England before coming
    to America

  b. L 841   c. L 842

Lawrence, William (165)
Meriden, Conn., 1831–34

Leddell, Joseph (166)
New York City, 1712–53

  a. L 853   b. L 854

  c. L 855   d. L 856

  e. L 455

Lee, Philip (167)
Beverly, Mass., ca. 1807–12

Lee, Richard, Sr. (168)
N. H. and Mass., 1788–1802
Springfield, Vt., 1802–1820

  a. L 408   b. L 409

  c. L 410   d. L 411

e. L 412   f. L 413   g. L 414

Lee, Richard, Jr. (169)
Springfield, Vt., 1795–1815 used (168), d,e,f,g, of
Richard Lee, Sr.

Lee and Creesy (170)
(Philip Lee and ——— Creesy)
Beverly, Mass., ca. 1807–12

  a. L 837

Leonard, Reed and Barton (171)
(Gustavus Leonard, Henry G. Reed, Charles E.
Barton)
Taunton, Mass., 1835–40

  a. Incised

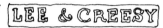

Leslie, Elkins (172)
Philadelphia, Pa., 1821–24
Brooklyn, N. Y., 1825

Lewis, Isaac C. (173)
Meriden, Conn., 1834–52

Lewis, I. C. and Co. (174)
(I. C. Lewis and D. B. Wells)
Meriden, Conn., 1839–52

Lewis and Cowles (175)
(I. C. Lewis and George Cowles)
East Meriden, Conn., 1834–36

Lightner, George (176)
Baltimore, Md., 1806–15

  a. L 566   b. L 567

Lincoln, —— (176)
Location unknown, after 1800

Locke, J. D. (177)
New York City, 1835–60

Love, I. (178)
Baltimore, Md., after 1830

"Love" (Lovebird mark) (179)
Pennsylvania, ca. 1750–93, attributed to Abraham Hasselberg (1750–79) or John Brunstrom (1781–93), both of Philadelphia

    a. L 868   b. L 869

    c. L 871

    also (46), b

Lowe, I. (180)
Location unknown, after 1800

Lyman, William W. (181)
Meriden, Conn., 1844–52

McEuen, Malcolm and Son (182)
(Malcolm and Duncan McEuen)
New York City, 1793–1803

    a. L 507   b. L 497

McQuilkin, William (183)
Philadelphia, Pa., 1839–53

    a.

Manning, E. B. (184)
Middletown, Conn., after 1840

Manning, Bowman & Co. (185)
Middletown, Conn., after 1850

Marston, —— (186)
Baltimore, Md., after 1830

Martine, James (187)
Fayetteville, N. C., ca. 1826–35

    a. L 875

Melville, David (188)
Newport, R. I., 1776–93

    a. L 317

    b. L 318

    c. L 319   d. L 320

    e. L 321 cast on
       porringer handle

    f. L 322   g. L 323   h. L 324

Melville, Samuel (189)
Newport, R. I., 1793–1800

137

Melville, S. and T. (190)
(Samuel and Thomas Melville, I or II)
Newport, R. I., 1793–1800

    a. L 326   b. L 327

Melville, Thomas, I (191)
Newport, R. I., 1793–96

    a. L 325 cast on
      porringer support

Melville, Thomas, II (192)
Newport, R. I., 1796–1824
New London, Conn., ca. 1820
  Used (191), a

    a. L 328, 329

Meriden Britannia Co. (193)
Meriden, Conn., 1852 and later

Michel, Andre (194)
New York City, 1742–52

    a. L 859   b. L 858

Miller, Josiah (195)
R. I. or Conn., 1700's

Mix, G. I. and Co. (196)
Yalesville, Conn., 1854–61 and later

Mix, Thomas (197)
Meriden, Conn., 1827 and later

Mix, William (198)
Prospect, Conn., 1827–50 and later

Morey and Ober (199)
(D. B. Morey and R. H. Ober)
Boston, Mass., 1852–55

  a.

Morey, Ober and Co. (200)
(D. B. Morey, R. H. Ober, Thomas Smith)
Boston, Mass., 1855–57

Morey and Smith (201)
(D. B. Morey and Thomas Smith)
Boston, Mass., 1857–60 and later

  a.

Munson, John (202)
Yalesville, Conn., 1846–52

  a.

Neal, I. (203)
Location unknown, 1842

Newell, J. C. (204)
Boston, Mass., 1853

Newell, Caldwell and Coffin (205)
(J. C. Newell, T. B. Caldwell, G. J. Coffin)
Boston, Mass., 1853

Nichols, O. (206)
Location unknown, early 19th century

138

Nott, William (207)
Middletown, Conn., 1809–17
Fayetteville, N. C., 1817–25

   a. L 450

Olcott, J. W. (208)
Baltimore, Md., ca. 1800

   a. L 565a

Ostrander, Charles (208)
New York City, 1848–54

Ostrander and Norris (209)
(Charles Ostrander and George Norris)
New York City, 1848–50

Palethorp, John H. (210)
Philadelphia, Pa., 1820–45

Palethorp, J. H. & Co. (211)
(J. H. Palethorp and Thomas Connell)
Philadelphia, Pa., 1839–41

Palethorp, Robert, Jr. (212)
Philadelphia, Pa., 1817–21

   a. L 559   b. L 560

   c. L 561

Palethorp and Connell (213)
(J. H. Palethorp and Thomas Connell)
Philadelphia, Pa., 1839–41

Palmer, W., II (214)
Location unknown, early 19th

Parker, Charles (215)
Wallingford, Conn., 1835–44

Parker, C. and Co. (216)
Wallingford, Conn., 1855–60 and later

Parker, Charles (217)
Meriden, Conn., before 1851, after 1859

Parker, J. G. (218)
Rochester, N. Y., 1840 and later

Parmenter, W. H. (219)
Location unknown, after 1840

Pennock, Samuel (220)
East Marlborough Township, Pa., 1785 and later

   a. L 598

Pennock, Simon (221)
East Marlborough Township, Pa., 1810–18, used
(220), a, of Samuel

Pierce, Samuel (222)
Greenfield, Mass., 1807–31

   a. L 407   b. L 406   c. L 405

Plumly, Charles (223)
Philadelphia, Pa., 1822–33

   a. L 873   b.

Plumly and Bidgood   (224)

(Charles Plumly and —— Bidgood)
Philadelphia, Pa., 1825

    a. L 562

Plumly and Felton   (225)

Location unknown, ca. 1840

Porter, Allen   (226)

Westbrook, Maine, 1830–38

    a.

Porter, Freeman   (227)

Westbrook, Maine, 1835–60 and later

Porter, James   (228)

Middletown, Conn., 1790–1803

    a. L 422   b. L 423

Potter, W.   (229)

Location unknown, after 1825

Putnam, James H.   (230)

Malden, Mass., 1830–55

    a.

Reed and Barton   (231)

(H. G. Reed and C. E. Barton)
Taunton, Mass., 1840 to present

Reich, John Philip   (232)

Salem, N. C., 1820–30

    a. L 571

Renton and Co.   (233)

New York City, after 1830

Richardson, B. & Son   (234)

Philadelphia, Pa., 1839

Richardson, George   (235)

Boston, Mass., 1818–28
Cranston, R. I., 1830–45

    a. L 310

    b.

Riley, Michael   (236)

Brooklyn, N. Y., 1830–38

Riley and Rogers   (237)

Brooklyn, N. Y., 1830–34

Rogers, Smith & Co.   (238)

(William Rogers and George W. Smith)
Hartford, 1856–62; New Haven, Conn. after 1862

Rust, H. N.   (239)

New York, ca. 1830–40

Rust, Samuel (240)
New York City, 1837–45

Sage, Timothy (241)
St. Louis, Mo., 1847–48

Sage and Beebe (242)
Location unknown, after 1840

Savage, William H. (243)
Middletown, Conn., 1837–40

Savage and Graham (244)
(William H. Savage and John B. Graham)
Middletown, Conn., 1837–38

Sellew and Company (245)
(Enos, Osman, and William Sellew)
Cincinnati, Ohio, 1832–60

a. **SELLEW & C⁰**
CINCINNATI

Semper Eadem (see Eadem, Semper)

Sheldon and Feltman (246)
(Smith Sheldon and J. C. Feltman, Jr.)
Albany, N. Y., 1847–48

a. Incised *SHELDON &*
FELTMAN.
ALBANY

b. Incised

Shoff, I (247)
Pennsylvania, late 18th century

Sickel and Shaw (248)
(H. G. Sickel and —— Shaw)
Philadelphia, Pa., 1849–50

Simpkins, Thomas (249)
Boston, Mass., 1726–66

a. L 288   b. L 289

Simpson, Samuel (250)
Yalesville, Conn., 1835–52

Simpson and Benham (251)
(Samuel Simpson and Darius Benham)
New York City, 1845–47

Skinner, John (252)
Boston, Mass., 1760–90

a. L 293

b. L 294

c. L 295

(97), e

Smith, Eben, Jr. (253)
Beverly, Mass., 1814–56

a. **E.SMITH**

Smith, George W. (254)
(See Smith & Feltman, Rogers, Smith & Co.)
Albany, N. Y., 1849–56
Hartford Conn., 1856–57

Smith, Ober and Co. (255)
(Thos. Smith, R. H. Ober, D. B. Morey)
Boston, Mass., 1849–52

Smith & Co. (256)
(Thos. Smith, D. B. Morey, Henry White)
Boston, Mass., 1847–49

a.

Smith and Feltman (257)
(Geo. W. Smith, J. C. Feltman, Sr.)
Albany, N. Y., 1849–52

a. Incised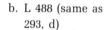

Smith and Morey (258)
(Thos. Smith and D. B. Morey)
Boston, Mass., 1841–42

Southmayd, Ebenezer (259)
Castleton, Vt., 1802–20

a. L 415   b. L 416

c. L 850

Stafford, Spencer (260)
Albany, N. Y., 1794–1830

a. L 517 S.STAFFORD

b. L 488 (same as 293, d)

c. L 520 ALBANY

d. L 521 incised

Stafford, Spencer and Co. (261)
Albany, N. Y., 1815–17

Stafford, S. & Co. (262)
Albany, N. Y., 1817–24

Stalkamp, J. H. & Co. (263)
Cincinnati, Ohio, 1853–56

Standish, Alexander (264)
see Armitages and Standish
Taunton, Mass., ca. 1835–40

Starr, William (265)
New York City, 1843–46

Stedman, Simeon (266)
Hartford, Conn., ca. 1818–25

Stimpson, James H. (267)
Baltimore, Md., 1851–57

Sykes, —— (268)
Location unknown, after 1840

B. G. S. & Co. (269)
Location unknown, ca. 1810–30

Taunton Britannia Maufacturing Co. (270)
Taunton, Mass., 1830–34

Thomas, John (271)
Philadelphia, Pa., 1841

Thompson, Andrew (272)
Albany, N. Y., 1811–17

a. L 866

b. L 865 THOMPSON

also used (260), c

Tillinghast, Paris J., Jr. **(273)**
Newport, R. I., ca. 1802–04

a. L 848

Tomlinson, Harvey **(274)**
Geneva, N. Y., 1843

Trask, Israel **(275)**
Beverly, Mass., ca. 1813–56

a.

Trask, Oliver **(276)**
Beverly, Mass., 1832–39

a.

Treadway, Amos **(277)**
Middletown, Conn., ca. 1760–90

a. L 384

(82), d, a

Vose and Co. **(278)**
Albany, N. Y., after 1840

Walker, —— **(279)**
New York City, after 1840

Wallace, R & Co. **(280)**
Wallingford, Conn., ca. 1838–55 and later

Ward, H. B. & Co. **(281)**
Wallingford, Conn., 1849 and later

Warren, Josiah **(282)**
Cincinnati, Ohio, 1821

Wayne, C. P. and Son **(283)**
Philadelphia, Pa., 1840–49

Webb, W. **(284)**
New York City, after 1810

Weekes, James **(285)**
New York City, after 1820
Brooklyn, N. Y., after 1830

a.

Weekes, J. & Co. **(286)**
Poughkeepsie, N. Y., 1833–35

a.

Whitfield, G. and J. **(287)**
New York City, 1836–65

Whitlock, John H. **(288)**
Troy, N. Y., 1847–56

Whitmore, Jacob **(289)**
Middletown, Conn., 1758–90

a. L 382 b. L 383

Whitmore and Francis **(290)**
(—— Whitmore and Daniel Francis)
Buffalo, N. Y., 1833

Wilcox, H. C. & Co. **(291)**
Meriden, Conn., ca. 1848–52

Wild(e)s, Thomas **(292)**
Philadelphia, Pa. 1829–33
New York, N. Y., 1833–40

a.

Will, Henry (293)

New York City, 1761–75, 1783–93
Albany, N. Y., 1776–83

a. L 485   b. L 486

c. L 487   d. L 488

e. L 489

f. L 491

g. L 492   h. L 490

Will, John (294)

New York City, 1752–74

a. L 474   b. L 483

c. L 475    d. L 478

e. L 479   f. L 480   g. L 481

h. L 484   i. L 482

Will, Philip (295)

New York City, 1766 and later
Philadelphia, Pa., 1763–87

a. L 476a

b. L 477a

c. same as (294),
c of John

Will, William (296)

Philadelphia, Pa., 1764–98

a. L 535   b. L 534

c. L 536

d. L 537

e. L 538, 539

f. L 540    g. L 541   h. L 542

144

Williams, Lorenzo L. (297)
Philadelphia, Pa., 1838–42

Williams, Otis (298)
Buffalo, N. Y., 1826–31

a. L 451

Williams and Simpson (299)
(Lorenzo L. Williams, Saml. Simpson)
Yalesville, Conn., 1837–38

Wood, H. N. (300)
Probably Taunton, Mass., ca. 1825–40

Woodbury, J. B. (301)
Beverly, Mass. ca., 1830–35
Philadelphia, Pa., 1835–38

a.   b.

c. J.B.WOODBURY

Woodbury and Colton (302)
(J. B. Woodbury, Oren Colton)
Philadelphia, Pa. 1835–38

a. WOODBURY & COLTON

Woodman Cook and Co. (303)
Portland, Maine, after 1830

Yale, Charles (304)
Wallingford, Conn., 1817–35

Yale, Hiram (305)
Wallingford, Conn., 1822–31

a. L 444

(86), a

Yale, H. & Co. (306)
(Hiram and Charles Yale)
Yalesville, Conn., Richmond, Va., 1824–35

a.

Yale, W. and S. (307)
(Wm. and Saml. Yale)
Meriden, Conn., 1813–20

a. L 440

Yale and Curtis (308)
(Henry Yale and Stephen Curtis)
New York City, 1858–67

a.

Yale and Henshaw (309)
(Edwin R. Yale, Jos. B. Henshaw)
Wallingford, Conn., 1835

Youle, George (310)
New York City, 1793–1828

Young, Peter (311)
New York City, 1775
Albany, N. Y., 1785–95

a. L 512

b. L 513

c. L 514

d. L 515

e. L 518

f. L 516

Initial Marks Cast on New England Porringers

These initial marks are found *cast* on the handles or support brackets of porringers of New England origin, made in the late eighteenth or early nineteenth century. The users of these marks are unknown.

a. E C   E C   L 572

b. C P   C P   L 573

c. S C   S G   L 574

d. WN   W N   L 575

e. I G   I C   L 576

   R G   R G   L 577

American Makers of Pewter or Britannia Without Reported Examples

The location of the shop and approximate working dates are given.

Name of Individual or Firm	Location of Shop	Approximate Working Dates
Alberti, Johann Philip	Philadelphia, Pa.	1754–80
Alberti and Horan	Philadelphia, Pa.	1758–64
Allaire, Anthony, Jr.	New York City	1815–21
Allison, John	Philadelphia, Pa.	1835–36
Andrews, Burr	Meriden, Conn.	1840–46
	New Haven, Conn.	1846
Andrews, John	Elizabeth City, Va.	1706
	Yorktown, Va.	1707
Archer, Benjamin	St. Louis, Mo.	1847
Austin, John	Boston, Mass.	1785
Badco(c)ke, Thomas	Philadelphia, Pa.	1707
Bailey, Timothy	Malden, Mass.	1830–40
Baldwin, Charles W.	New Britain, Conn.	1831
Ballantyne, John	Norfolk, Va.	1763–69
Barton, Charles E.	Taunton, Mass.	1835–67
Bass, Daniel	Fayetteville, N. C.	1807–ca. 1813
Beastall	New York City	1825–26
Benedict, Lewis	Albany, N. Y.	1815–24
Benham, Darius	New York City	1845–47
Benham and Whitney	New York City	1849
Bennett, Edward	New York City	1760

Name of Individual or Firm	Location of Shop	Approximate Working Dates
Bidwell, Solomon	Auburn, N. Y.	1842–43
Bilbro, John	Surry County, Va.	1773 and earlier
Billings and Danforth	Providence, R. I.	1798–1801
Bird, James	New York City	1820–21
Bland, James	Westchester County, N. Y.	1761
Blaun, James	Westchester County, N. Y.	1759
Blin, Peter	Boston, Mass.	1757–59
Bliss, Jonathan & Co.	Brooklyn, N. Y.	1822–23
Boardman, J. D.	Hartford, Conn.	1828
Boardman, Sherman	Hartford, Conn.	1810–50
Bokee, William	Brooklyn, N. Y.	1817–24
Boker, William	Philadelphia, Pa.	1800
Bouis, John	Baltimore, Md.	1829–34
Bouis, John and Son	Baltimore, Md.	1831–32
Bouis, Joseph	Baltimore, Md.	1834
Bouzigues, ——	Philadelphia, Pa.	1810
Bowditch, Capt.	Salem, Mass.	1814
Bowles, Samuel	Boston, Mass.	1787–88
Bowman, Nathaniel	Charlestown, Mass.	1806–14
Bowman, ——	Middletown, Conn.	After 1850
Bradford, John	Boston, Mass.	1784–88
Bradford and McEuen	New York City	1772–85
Brainard	Cobalt, Conn.	1840 or later
Brigden, John	Albany, N. Y.	1823–25
Brooks, David S.	Hartford, Conn.	1828
Browe and Dougherty	Newark, N. J.	1845–53
Brower, C. S.	New Orleans, La.	1822
Bumste(a)d, Thomas	Roxbury, Mass.	1640–43
	Boston, Mass.	1643–1677
Burroughs, Thomas	Boston, Mass.	ca. 1684
	New York City	ca. 1685–1703
Burroughs, Thomas, Jr.	New York City	ca. 1705–1712
Butler and Perkins	Boston, Mass.	1852–53
Caldwell, T. B.	Boston, Mass.	1853
Camp, William E.	Middletown, Conn.	1849
Campbell, John	Annapolis, Md.	1749
Campbell, Mungo	Philadelphia, Pa.	1749–52
	Norfolk, Va.	1756–64

Name of Individual or Firm	Location of Shop	Approximate Working Dates
Carter, Samuel	Boston, Mass.	1712–47
Clark(e), Jonas	Boston, Mass.	1715–37
Clark(e), Thomas	Boston, Mass.	1674–1720
Coffin, G. J.	Boston, Mass.	1853
Comer, John	Boston, Mass.	1674–1721
Comer, John, Jr.	Boston, Mass.	1700–1706
Cone, S. L.	Meriden, Conn.	1849
Connell, Thomas	Philadelphia, Pa.	1829–1840
Cook	Portland, Maine	After 1850
Corne, Anthony	Charleston, S. C.	1735
Cottam, Shub(a)el	Albany, N. Y.	1815
Couch, Ira	Meriden, Conn.	1830–45
Cowles, George C.	Meriden, Conn.	1834–36
Cox, William	Philadelphia, Pa.	1715–21
Crossman, William W.	Taunton, Mass.	1824–27
Curtis, Stephen	New York, N. Y.	1858–67
Curtiss, Edwin E.	Meriden, Conn.	1838–45
Curtiss, Enos. H.	Meriden, Conn.	1845–49
Curtiss and Lyman	Meriden, Conn.	1846
Danforth, Job	Providence, R. I.	1798–1801
Danforth, Jonathan	Middletown, Conn.	1789–94
Danforth, Jonathan & William	Middletown, Conn.	1790–94
Danforth, Thomas (the first)	Taunton, Mass.	1727–33
	Norwich, Conn.	1733–ca. 1775
Danforth, Thomas (1st) and John	Norwich, Conn.	ca. 1762–73
Danforth, Thomas (4th)	Philadelphia, Pa.	1812
	Augusta, Georgia	1818
Danforth and Hamlin	Middletown, Conn.	ca. 1767–73
Davis, Edmund	Philadelphia, Pa.	1720–21
Derby, Albert H.	Middletown, Conn.	1835–50
	New Haven, Conn.	1851–54
Derby, Thomas S., Jr.	Middletown, Conn.	1840–50
Derby, Thomas S. and Son	Middletown, Conn.	1849
Digg(e)s, William	New York City	1801–02
Dolbeare, David	Boston, Mass.	ca. 1736–ca. 1770
Dolbeare, James	Boston, Mass.	1727–40
Dougherty, William M.	Newark, N. J.	1845–49

Name of Individual or Firm	Location of Shop	Approximate Working Dates
Durninger, Daniel	Boston, Mass.	1722–23
Edgell, William	Boston, Mass.	1724
Eggleston and Bass	Fayetteville, N. C.	1807–12
Ellison, John	Philadelphia, Pa.	1837
Elton, William	Wallingford, Conn.	1849–50
Engel, Gottlieb	Philadelphia, Pa.	1858
Estabrook(e), Richard	Boston, Mass.	1720–21
Everett, James	Philadelphia, Pa.	1716–17
Fairbanks, Jonathan	Sherborn, Mass.	1683
Feltman, J. C., Jr.	Albany, N. Y.	1847–48
Fields, Philip	New York City	1799
Flagg, David	Boston, Mass.	1750–72
Fletcher, Thomas	Philadelphia, Pa.	1837–41
Foote, Henry C.	Wallingford, Conn.	1850
Foote, James and Co.	Wallingford, Conn.	1850–51
Francis, Thomas	Boston, Mass.	1718
Frary, James A.	Meriden, Conn.	1845–49
Frary and Benham	Meriden, Conn.	1849
Frary and Boardman	Meriden, Conn.	1837–38
Frink, Prentice	Stonington, Conn.	1792
Garey and Hammond	Baltimore, Md.	1819
Geanty, Lewis	Baltimore, Md.	1800–03
Gehring, John G.	Baltimore, Md.	1824
George, Anthony, Jr.	Philadelphia, Pa.	1839–47
Gooch, John	Portsmouth, N. H.	1782
Graham, Jasper	Middletown, Conn.	1837
Graham, John B.	Middletown, Conn.	1837–38
Grame (or Greames), Samuel	Boston, Mass.	1639–45
Graves, Richard	Salem, Mass.	1635–67
Green, Andrew	Boston, Mass.	1773–98
Green, Jonas	Boston, Mass.	1786–87
Green, Samuel, Jr.	Boston, Mass.	1826–35
Green, Thomas	Boston, Mass.	1740–94
Green, Thomas, Jr.	Boston, Mass.	1769–86
Green, Timothy	Boston, Mass.	1780–82
Green and Austin	Boston, Mass.	1812–17
Green and Richardson	Boston, Mass.	1818
Greene and Belcher	New London, Conn.	1787

Name of Individual or Firm	Location of Shop	Approximate Working Dates
Grindell (or Grennell), Thomas	New York City	1789–91
Griswold and Couch	Meriden, Conn.	1830
Haldane, James	Philadelphia, Pa.	1765–69
	Norfolk, Va.	1772
	Petersburg, Va.	1776
Hall, Almer	Wallingford, Conn.	1827–34
		1847–60 and later
Hall, Franklin D.	Hartford, Conn.	1840
	Philadelphia, Pa.	1842–57
Hall, John H.	Middletown, Conn.	1815–17
Hamlin and Jones	Providence, R. I.	1774–81
Hammond, Joseph	Baltimore, Md.	1819
Harner, George	New York City	1761
Hasselberg, Abraham	Bethlehem, Pa.	1750–58
	Wilmington, Del.	1759–ca. 1762
	Philadelphia, Pa.	ca. 1762–79
Hattersley, Joseph	Newark, N. J.	1850–51
Hattersley, William	Newark, N. J.	1849–61
Hattersley and son J.	Newark, N. J.	1856–61
Hendricks, Francis G.	Charleston, S. C.	1771–84
Henley (Hendley), Peter	Rowan County, N. C.	1775
Henry, Andrew	Orange County, N. Y.	1761
Henshaw, Joseph B.	Wallingford, Conn.	1835
Henshaw and Hamlin	Hartford, Conn.	1767–c. 1768
Hera, Christian	Philadelphia, Pa.	1791–1817
Hera, John	Philadelphia, Pa.	1800–12
Hera, John, Second	Philadelphia, Pa.	1817–21
Hill, John	New York City	1846–48
Hillsburgh, Charles	New York City	1837
Holyoke, John	Boston, Mass.	1706–60
Horan, Johann Christian	Philadelphia, Pa.	1758–86
Horsewell, William	New York City	1705–09
House, Edwin	Hartford, Conn.	1841–46
Humiston, Hiram	Troy, N. Y.	1850–53
Hunter, George	Troy, N. Y.	1831
Isly, Joseph	New York City	1715
Jackson, Isaac	New Garden Township, Chester County, Pa.	1774–1807

Name of Individual or Firm	Location of Shop	Approximate Working Dates
Jackson, Jonathan	Boston, Mass.	1695–1736
Jagger, Daniel H.	Hartford, Conn.	1844–46
Jagger, James H.	Hartford, Conn.	1843
Jagger, Walter W.	Hartford, Conn.	1839–46
Janney, N. E. and Co.	St. Louis, Mo.	1845
Jennings, Theodore	Location unknown	1775
Johnson, Elijah	Baltimore, Md.	1822–23
Johnson, G. W.	Greenfield, Mass.	1834
Johnson, Hall and Co.	Middletown, Conn.	1815–17
Johnson and Nott	Middletown, Conn.	1817–18
	Fayetteville, N. C.	1818–19
Jones, Daniel	Boston, Mass.	1705
Jones, Gershom and Sons	Providence, R. I.	1806–07
Kehler (or Koehler), Adam	Philadelphia, Pa.	1779–83
Kiersted, Luke	New York City	1802–14
Kilbourn and Porter	Baltimore, Md.	1814–16
Knapp, Elijah	New York City	1796–97
Kneeland, Edward	Boston, Mass.	1768–91
Knowles, Henry	Providence, R. I.	1826–31
Lafetra and Allaire	New York City	1816
Lake, John D.	Middletown, Conn.	1850
Langshaw, Thomas	Philadelphia, Pa.	1689
	Chester County, Pa.	ca. 1693–96
Lathbury, John	Virginia	1655
Leddell, Joseph, Jr.	New York City	ca. 1740–54
Lees and Beastall	New York City	1825–26
Leonard, Gustavus	Taunton, Mass.	1837–45
Leonard, Horatio	Taunton, Mass.	1830–37
Leonard, Zephaniah	Taunton, Mass.	1829–32
Lewis and Curtiss	East Meriden, Conn.	1836–39
Lewis and Holt	Meriden, Conn.	1831
Locke and Carter	New York City	1837–45
Lucas, Ivory	New London, Conn.	1732–47
	Ogles Town, Del.	1747–48
Lyell, David	New York City	1714
Lyman and Couch	Meriden, Conn.	1844–45
McEuen, Duncan	New York City	1793–1803
McEuen, Malcolm	New York City	1765–1803

Name of Individual or Firm	Location of Shop	Approximate Working Dates
McIlmoy, John	Philadelphia, Pa.	1793
Mann, William	Boston, Mass.	1690–1738
Manning, Thaddeus	Middletown, Conn.	1849
Marshall, Joseph	New York City	1821–22
Maton, Marcus	Hartford, Conn.	1828
Melville, Andrew	Newport, R. I.	1804–10
Melville, William L.	Newport, R. I.	1807–10
Merryfield, Robert	New York City	1760
Metcalf, Michael	Dedham, Mass.	1691
Michel, Andre	New York City	1795–97
Minze, James	Albany, N. Y.	1794–96
Mix, Garry I.	Wallingford, Conn.	ca. 1845–54
	Yalesville, Conn.	1854–61 and later
Mix, William	Meriden area, Conn.	ca. 1845 and later
Molineux, George	New York City	1848–54
Moore, Luke	Philadelphia, Pa.	1819–22
Morey, David B.	Boston, Mass.	1841–45
		1847–64 and later
	Charlestown, Mass.	1845
Morgan, Henry	Groton, Conn.	1849
Nexsen, Edmund	New York City	1818–19
Norris, George	New York City	1848–50
Norsworthy, John	Norfolk, Va.	1771
North, John	Augusta, Ga.	1818–23
North and Rowe	Augusta, Ga.	1818–23
Northey, David	Salem, Mass.	1732–78
Northey, William	Lynn, Mass.	1764–1804
Nott, William	Philadelphia, Pa.	1812
Nott, Babcock and Johnson	Middletown, Conn.	1817
Ober, R. H.	Boston, Mass.	1849–56
Palethorp, Robert	Philadelphia, Pa.	1822–26
Palethorp, R. & J. H.	Philadelphia, Pa.	1820–25
Paschall, Thomas	Philadelphia, Pa.	1686–1718
Pavey, Adam	Spotsylvania Co., Va.	1756
Pavey, George	Boston, Mass.	1733
Peale, (Peal, Peel or Piel), Henry	Philadelphia, Pa.	1820–22 and 1830–33
	Brooklyn, N. Y.	1822–26

Name of Individual or Firm	Location of Shop	Approximate Working Dates
Pearse, Robert	New York City	1792
Pelton, F. W. & O. Z.	Middletown, Conn.	ca. 1852–60
Pelton, William	Portland, Conn.	1849–c. 1852
Perkins, Daniel	Boston, Mass.	1852–53
Pierce, John J.	Greenfield, Mass.	1833 and later
Pierce, J. & S.	Greenfield, Mass.	1834 and later
Pierce, Samuel, Jr.	Greenfield, Mass.	1833 and later
Pierce and Johnson	Greenfield, Mass.	1833–34
Pierce and Son	Greenfield, Mass.	ca. 1811–21
Piercy, Robert	New York City	1792–97
Plumly, Charles	Providence, R. I.	1829
	Middletown, Conn.	1844–48
Pomroy, William C.	Cincinnati, Ohio	1853–56
Porter, A. & F.	Westbrook Maine	1835–38
Porter, Jephtha	Baltimore, Md.	1814–16
Porter, Robert	Caln Township, Chester Co., Pa.	ca. 1770–85
Raisin, George	Boston, Mass.	1718–28
Rand, Edward	Newburyport, Mass.	1774
Randle (or Randall), Joseph	Boston, Mass.	1738–39 and earlier
	Providence, R. I.	1744–50
Rease, Francis	Philadelphia, Pa.	1820–22
Reed, Henry G.	Taunton, Mass.	1835–80 and later
Reich, J. & P.	Salem, N. C.	1829
Richardson, Francis B.	Providence, R. I.	1847–48
Richardson, George B.	Providence, R. I.	1847–48
Richardson, Jabez	Baltimore, Md.	1817–18
Rodgers, John	Philadelphia, Pa.	1839–40
Rogers, ——	Brooklyn, N. Y.	1830–34
Rowe, Adna S.	Augusta, Ga.	1818–28
Rust, John N. and Samuel	New York City	1842–45
Rust, Leonard M.	New York City	1849
Sage, T. and Co.	St. Louis, Mo.	1847
Savage, William	Middletown, Conn.	1838–39
Scull, Benjamin	Philadelphia, Pa.	1810–11
Seip, Jacob	Philadelphia, Pa.	1820–22
Seltzer, Abraham	Philadelphia, Pa.	1793
Shaw, ——	Philadelphia, Pa.	1849–50
Shrimpton, Henry	Boston, Mass.	1639–66

Name of Individual or Firm	Location of Shop	Approximate Working Dates
Sickel, H. G.	Philadelphia, Pa.	1849–53
Sizer, Amasa	Middletown, Conn.	1799
Smith, Aaron	Philadelphia, Pa.	1736–37
Smith, James E.	Maryland?	After 1775
Smith, Thomas	Boston, Mass.	1700–42
Smith, Thomas	Boston, Mass.	1841–62
Smith, Thomas and Co.	Boston, Mass.	1842–47
Smith, William R.	Middletown, Conn.	1848
Smith & Co.	Albany, N. Y.	1853–56
Spencer, George B.	Albany, New York	1815–17
Spencer, Thomas	Albany, New York	1815
Stafford, Benedict and Co.	Albany, New York	1824
Stafford, Hallenbake	Albany, New York	1815–24
Stafford, Spencer, Jr.	Albany, New York	1817–24
Stafford and Minze	Albany, N. Y.	1794–96
Staffords, Rogers and Co.	Albany, New York	1814–15
Stanley, Samuel G.	Brooklyn, N. Y.	1826–29
Stoddart, Fredrick	Philadelphia, Pa.	1833
Sumner, William F.	New York City	1846–51
Thornton, John	Philadelphia, Pa.	1774
Tyler, John	Boston, Mass.	1720–56
Tymiesen, Sebastian	Albany, New York	1815–17
Van Dalsam, John	New York City	1775
Van Kleeck, Peter	New York City	1775
Vartklop's Britannia Ware	Neward, N. J.	1831
Wadsworth, Lester	Hartford, Conn.	1838
Ward, Reuben	Philadelphia, Pa.	1825
Warner, James M.	Providence, R. I.	1828–48
Warren, John B.	Boston, Mass.	1825–28
Wells, D. B.	Meriden, Conn.	1839–52
Wendeln, John F.	Cincinnati, Ohio	1853–55
West, William A.	Taunton, Mass.	1828–30
White, Henry	Boston, Mass.	1842–49
White, James	New York City	1821–34
Whitfield, George B.	New York City	1828–65
Whitlock, J. H. & Co.	Troy, N. Y.	1854–56
Whitmore, Lewis	Rocky Hill, Conn.	1841
Whitney, Chauncey	Albany, N. Y.	1822

Name of Individual or Firm	Location of Shop	Approximate Working Dates
Whitney, ——	New York City	1849
Will, Christian	New York City	1770–89
Will, George W.	Philadelphia, Pa.	1799–1807
Willett, Edward	Upper Marlboro, Md.	1692–1743
Willett, Mary	Upper Marlboro, Md.	1773
Willett, William	Upper Marlboro, Md.	1744–72
Williams, Richard	Stepney, Conn.	1793–1800
Willis, Thomas	Philadelphia, Pa.	1829–33
Wilson, Joseph	New York City	1775
Witherle (or Weatherly), Joshua	Boston, Mass.	1784–93
Wolfe, John	Philadelphia, Pa.	1801
Wyer, Simon	Philadelphia, Pa.	1740–52
E. W.	Virginia	18th century
Yale, Burrage	South Reading, Mass.	1808–35
Yale, C. and S.	Wallingford, Conn. Richmond, Va.	1817–23
Yale, Henry	New York City	1858–67
Yale, Samuel	Meriden, Conn.	1813–20
Yale, Selden	Wallingford, Conn. Richmond, Va.	1817–23
Yale, William	Meriden, Conn.	1813–1820
	New York City	1830–32
Youle, Thomas	New York City	1813–19
Young, Abraham	New York City	1796

Bibliography

General

Bulletin of the Pewter Collectors' Club of America, Bulletins No. 21–64.

Cotterell, Howard H., *Old Pewter*, London, B. T. Batsford, Ltd., 1929.

Goyne, Nancy A., "Britannia in America," *Winterthur Portfolio II, 1965*, Winterthur, Delaware, The Henry Francis Dupont Museum, 1965.

Jacobs, Carl, *Guide to American Pewter*, New York, The McBride Co., 1957.

Kerfoot, J. B., *American Pewter*, Boston, Houghton Mifflin Co., 1924.

Laughlin, Ledlie I., *American Pewter, Its Makers and Their Marks*, Vols. I & II, Boston, Houghton Mifflin, 1940; Vol. III, Barre, Mass., Barre, 1971.

1

Cotterell, Howard H., "The Evolution of the Trencher," *Antiques*, Vol. XVII, No. 1, January 1934.

Cummings, Abbott, ed., *Rural Household Inventories (1675–1775)*, Boston, The Society for the Preservation of New England Antiquities, 1964.

Decatur, Stephen, "English Pottery and the American Cotton Trade," *American Collector*, June 1940.

Dow, George Francis

    Arts and Crafts in New England, Topsfield, Mass., The Wayside Press, 1927; "House Furnishings in Salem in 1685," *Old-Time New England, The Bulletin of the Society for the Preservation of New England Antiquities*, Vol. XIII, No. 3, January 1923, Serial #31;

    "Notes on the Use of Pewter in Massachusetts During the Seventeenth Century," *Old-Time New England*, Vol. XIV, No. 1, July 1923.

Earle, Alice M., *China Collecting in America*, New York, Charles Scribner's Sons, 1892.

Hanna, Agnes McCulloch, "Two Antique Pewter Hanukkah Lamps," *American Collector*, IX, No. 1, February 1940.

Michaelis, Ronald F., *British Pewter,* London, Ward Lock & Co., Limited, 1969.

Peal, Christopher A., *British Pewter and Britannia Metal,* London, John Gifford, 1971.

Shelley, Roland J. A., "Some Early Inventories of Pewter in Country Houses," *Appollo,* Vol. XLVI, No. 272, October 1947.

Symonds, R. W., "The English Export Trade in Furniture to Colonial America," Part II, *Antiques,* Vol. XXVIII, No. 4, October 1935.

2

Bishop, J. Leander, *A History of American Manufactures from 1608 to 1860, Vol III,* Philadelphia, Edward Young & Co., 1868.

Gibb, George S., *The Whitesmiths of Taunton, A History of Reed and Barton,* Cambridge, Mass., The Harvard University Press, 1946.

Hinckley, C. I., "Everyday Actualities—No. VIII," *Godey's Lady's Book,* Vol. XVI, March 1853.

Kauffman, Henry J., *The American Pewterer,* Camden, New Jersey, Thomas Nelson & Sons, 1970.

Swain, Charles V., "Interchangeable Parts in Early American Pewter" *Antiques,* Vol. LXXXIII, No. 2, February 1963.

3 & 4

An Exhibition of Connecticut Pewter, The New Haven Colony Historical Society, April 1963.

Graham, John M., *American Pewter,* The Brooklyn Museum, 1949.

Hood, Graham
  American Silver, New York, Praeger, 1971.
  "American Pewter," *Yale University Art Gallery Bulletin,* Vol. 30, No. 3, Fall 1965.

Michaelis, Ronald, "English Pewter Porringers," parts I, II, III, IV, *Apollo,* Vol. L #295–298, July, August, September, and October 1949.

Pewter in America 1650–1900, Catalog of Exhibition Oct. 6–Nov. 3, 1968. The Currier Gallery of Art, Manchester, N. H.

Raymond, Percy E., "William Calder, A Transition Pewterer," *Antiques,* Vol. XXX, #5, November 1936.

Watkins, Laura Woodside, "George Richardson, Pewterer," *Antiques,* Vol XXXI, No. 4, April 1937.

Webber, John W., "Roswell Gleason," *Antiques,* August 1931.

Woodside, Charles L., and Laura Woodside, "Three Maine Pewterers," *Antiques,* Vol. 22, No. 1, July 1932.

5

Freeman, Larry, *New Light on Old Lamps,* Century House, Watkins Glen, N. Y., 1968.

Matthews, L. Harrison, "A Note on Whaling," *A History of Technology,* ed. By Singer, Holmyard, Hall, and Williams, Vol. 4, Oxford at the Clarendon Press, Great Britain, 1958.

McFarland, W. A., "Shedding Light on Pewter Lamps," *The Pewter Collector's Club of America Bulletin,* Vol. 4, No. 10.

Sanderson, Ivin T., *Flickering Flames,* Charles E. Tuttle Co., Rutland, Vermont, 1958.

Thwing, L. L., "Lamp Oils and Other Illuminants," *Old Time New England,* Vol. XXIII, No. 2, Serial No. 70, October 1932.

Watkins, Malcolm C., "Lighting Devices," *The Concise Encyclopedia of American Antiques,* edited by Helen Comstock, pp. 355–363, Hawthorn Books, Inc., New York.

Watkins, Malcolm C., "The Whale Oil Burner; Its Invention and Development," *Antiques Magazine,* Vol. XXVII, No. 4, April 1935.

6

Application of Science in Examination of Works of Art, Proceedings of the Seminar: September 7–16, 1965, Research Laboratory, Museum of Fine Arts, Boston, Mass.

Plenderleith, H. J., and Werner A. E. A., *The Conservation of Antiquities and Works of Art,* Second Edition, London, Oxford University Press, 1971.

Index